York St John College
Fountains Learning Centre

Successful Interviews
Every Time

If you want to know how . . .

Passing Psychometric Tests
Know what to expect and get the job you want

The Job Application Handbook
*Sell yourself to an employer using proven strategies and
effective techniques*

Returning to Work
How to work out what you want and then go out and get it

The Ten Career Commandments
*Equip yourself with the 10 most important skills to move
up the career ladder*

Passing That Interview
Your step-by-step guide to coming out on top

howtobooks

Please send for a free copy of the latest catalogue to:

How To Books
3 Newtec Place, Magdalen Road
Oxford OX4 1RE, United Kingdom
e-mail: info@howtobooks.co.uk
http://www.howtobooks.co.uk

Successful Interviews Every Time

Second edition

Dr ROB YEUNG

howtobooks

Published by How To Books Ltd,
3 Newtec Place, Magdalen Road,
Oxford OX4 1RE, United Kingdom.
Tel: (01865) 793806. Fax: (01865) 248780.
email: info@howtobooks.co.uk
http://www.howtobooks.co.uk

First edition 2002
Second edition 2004
Reprinted 2004

British Library Cataloguing in Publication Data.
A catalogue record for this book is available from
the British Library.

Produced for How To Books by Deer Park Productions, Tavistock
Edited by Diana Brueton
Cover design by Baseline Arts Ltd, Oxford
Typeset by Kestrel Data, Exeter, Devon
Printed and bound by Cromwell Press Ltd, Trowbridge, Wiltshire

NOTE: The material contained in this book is set out in good
faith for general guidance and no liability can be accepted
for loss or expense incurred as a result of relying in particular
circumstances on statements made in the book. Laws and
regulations are complex and liable to change, and readers should
check the current position with the relevant authorities before
making personal arrangements.

Contents

Preface

to the Second edition

Do you ever feel frustrated that you are not putting yourself across to the very best of your ability in interviews? I wrote the first edition of this book because in my job as an interviewer on behalf of companies big and small, I have seen too many candidates who were just not doing themselves justice. And it is always a shame because in most cases it is something that they could quite easily resolve.

Interviews come in all shapes and sizes. There could be just a single interviewer or a panel of interviewers. You might be put at your ease and asked a handful of straightforward questions. Or you might be subjected to a traumatic interview designed to wear you down.

You might be ready for just one interview lasting a couple of hours, but what if you are faced with a dozen interviews each lasting an hour? And what if you are given a case study interview, a presentation to prepare, or even a group discussion to contend with?

No matter, this book covers them all. Filled with just about every question that you might be asked and examples of proven answers, it will help you prepare responses that are perfect for you. Never be caught out by any interview question ever again.

The job market continues to evolve – interviewers are sharpening up their skills and asking even more complicated questions to weed out poor candidates – so I have updated many of the questions in this second edition. And I have found that even more interviewers are using the competency-based interview technique, so I have particularly expanded the chapter that deals with it in this edition.

Perhaps you want to work in the private or public sector. Maybe you want to join a global company or a local firm. Are you are a graduate looking for your first job or a senior executive searching for a better job? Whatever you are looking for, you can be confident of making a great impression and acing that interview. Prepare to stand out from the other candidates, and land the job you want.

So read this book and be confident in yourself. And if you ever come across any particularly devious interviewer tricks or questions, feel free to email me and I might include it in the next edition of the book.

Rob Yeung

robyeung@robyeung.freeserve.co.uk

Doing Your Homework

In this Chapter . . .

◆ Getting to grips with your own skills
◆ Deciphering job adverts
◆ Researching the employer
◆ Making contact by telephone
◆ How to practise for interviews

Being invited to an interview is a significant step. Many companies see hundreds of CVs or application forms and only shortlist a handful of candidates to go for interview. You should pat yourself on the back for getting this far. So don't mess it up now.

Research and preparation are 50% of the hard work to getting the job. Many interviewers often say that candidates let themselves down almost immediately by not knowing enough about the company.

This chapter covers exactly what you need to know before you walk through the door to that interview.

YOU HAVE ALL THE SKILLS AND EXPERIENCE YOU NEED FOR INTERVIEWS

No matter how relaxed and informal an interview might be, it is not simply a conversation or a 'chat'. It is an opportunity to sell yourself and convince the interviewer that you are the best person for the job.

So think of an interview as a sales pitch. And before you can do your sales pitch, you must understand your product – yourself. Before you carry on with the rest of the book, take a notepad and jot down some thoughts to the following questions:

◆ What are the three biggest achievements of your career?
◆ What are you most proud of outside of your work?
◆ What are your goals in your career? What would you like to get out of your next job move?
◆ Why should an employer want you to work for them?

Do take the time – even if it is only 20 minutes – to think about these questions. Time spent now will make it much easier for you to respond competently to the many questions that interviewers might throw at you later.

Transferable skills

You have probably already heard that employers are always looking for particular skills. So just take a few minutes to rate yourself on a scale of 1 to 10 (where 1 = 'terrible', 5 = 'average', and 10 = 'exceptional') on the following key skills:

◆ **Communication** – how well can you get the message across to other people – either by writing reports and documents, talking informally with them, or perhaps giving formal presentations?

◆ **Cooperation** – can you get on with other people? Can you work as part of a team? How well do you handle conflict and disagreement with other people?

◆ **Persuasion** – how good are you at influencing other people and getting them to change their minds? Can you convince and win people over to do what you want them to do?

◆ **Problem solving** – how good are you at analysing situations, weighing up the pros and cons, and choosing a course of action to make things better?

◆ **Self-motivation** – how driven are you? Compared with other people, would you say that you are dedicated about your work? Are you enthusiastic and energetic? And can other people rely on you to get the job done?

◆ **Effectiveness** – how successful have you been in making a difference to your company? Can you think of examples when you have saved the company money, reduced the time it takes to do something, or improved efficiency?

◆ **Business awareness** – how much do you know about your industry? Do you know who the main companies in your sector are? Do you know what the differences between the competitors in the sector are?

Now keep the answers to these questions in mind as you read through the example questions and model answers in Chapters 3 to 7.

STUDY THE JOB ADVERT FOR CRUCIAL INFORMATION

Always keep a copy of the original job advert. When you are invited to an interview, take a look at the key words and phrases in the advert to help you to **figure out what the key skills and characteristics for the job are**. Then you will be able to prepare for the questions that the interviewer is most likely to ask you.

For example, take a look at the following job advert:

Europe's premier **industrial components** company Bayern McFadden is seeking a **graduate-calibre** manager to **revitalise** its UK **manufacturing** division. Successful candidates will have significant experience of **leading teams** to **turn around business performance**. You will **work alongside continental European managers** to **deliver results**. **MBA would be an advantage**. Considerable salary and bonus for the right candidate. For an application form, please contact Janet Baxendale on 030 7000 8080.

Reading the job advert above, we can make certain deductions about the key skills that may be involved and therefore the questions they might ask:

◆ The fact that the company describes itself as working in 'industrial components' and 'manufacturing' immediately throws up two questions that an interviewer might ask. Firstly, "Do you have any relevant experience in this sector?" Secondly, if you do not have directly relevant experience, "Why are you interested in working in this sector?"

◆ 'Graduate calibre' does not mean that you necessarily need to be a graduate. If you managed to get an interview, then obviously you have the right experience. But you may be asked questions about the reasons you did not go to university and how you have developed your skills over the years.

◆ The words 'revitalise' and phrase 'turn around business performance' indicate that the division is not doing very well. So be ready to answer questions such as: "In your career so far, can you give me an example of how you have improved the performance of a business?" and, "If we offered you the job, what steps would you take first to tackle the performance of the division?"

◆ 'Leading teams' suggests that the interviewer might ask a question such as: "When working with a new team, how do you go about building your relationships with the team?"

◆ The phrase 'work alongside continental European managers' throws up questions about your language skills and previous experience of working across cultural boundaries.

◆ The phrase 'deliver results' suggests that you are able to set targets, work to deadlines, and achieve measurable benefits.

◆ Finally, if you do not have an MBA, then you must be able to give a credible reason why you should still be considered for the job if you do not possess an MBA or some similar business qualification.

Here is another job advert:

Gold Asset Management Limited is looking for a **personal assistant** to support a busy Managing Director. You will schedule appointments, **deal with travel arrangements** for his frequent international trips and use the **latest computer software** to prepare presentations for him. You will also manage occasional **projects in liaison with external clients**. To be successful in this role, you will need to be **highly self-motivated**. Central London location. £ dependent on experience.

Email: sushma.meera@gold-assetmanagement.co.uk

So what does this advert say about the questions that you could be asked?

- ◆ As the job is looking for a 'personal assistant', you would need to be ready to talk about your previous experience in other roles as a personal assistant. The interviewer might ask: "What have your previous bosses been like in the past?" or "What kind of person do you most enjoy working with?"
- ◆ 'Deal with travel arrangements' suggests that you might need to be able to respond to questions such as: "Your Managing Director needs to be in Paris on Friday afternoon. It is now Thursday afternoon and the airline has just rung to tell you that they have had to cancel the flights. What would you do now?"
- ◆ Be ready to talk about your experience of the 'latest

computer software'. What packages are you familiar with?

◆ The phrase 'projects in liaison with external clients' actually thows up two separate areas to cover. What is your experience of having managed projects? And be ready to talk about examples of how you have dealt with the demands of clients.

◆ Since the advert is looking for someone who is 'highly self-motivated', would you be able to provide examples of how you have motivated yourself at work?

Hopefully you should now understand the need to break down the job advert and think about possible questions. Chapters 3 to 7 will give you some advice on how to construct good responses.

RESEARCH IS CRITICAL TO UNDERSTAND YOUR PROSPECTIVE EMPLOYER

Employers like to feel that candidates have made an effort to find out about them. And the more information you have, the easier it will be for you to tailor your interview responses to show the interviewer that you are the perfect person for the job.

At a minimum, you should be able to establish the following:

◆ What sort of business are they in and what are their current services or products?

◆ What are the company's vision, mission and values?

◆ What is their strategy for the future? What plans or investments do they have lined up or going forwards?

◆ Approximately how many staff does the organisation employ? Are they a very large or a very small employer?

◆ Who are their competitors?

In your preparation, you should read ravenously. Any snippet you pick up could make the difference – showing that you have invested time and effort in understanding the company.

Study any available literature

Look at the company's corporate literature and their website. You could also:

◆ Ask friends, family, and acquaintances for information about the company. Often, they may know people who know something about the company. Or, even better, they may know someone who could speak to you – perhaps on the telephone or over a coffee – to give you inside gossip and news about the company.

◆ Visit a retail outlet, shop or showroom – if the company has any. If you can buy, try, or get a feel for the company's products or services before an interview, you will give yourself a significant advantage.

Using the Internet

The Internet provides easy access to a large volume of information about employers. Three of the best websites are:

◆ **www.ft.com** – the website of the *Financial Times*. You can enter a company name into a search box and it will return with a comprehensive list of articles w information about your target company.

◆ **www.newsunlimited.co.uk** – the website of *The Guardian* newspaper. This often has better coverage of smaller businesses, non-profit organisations and public sector employers.

◆ **www.carol.com** – Company Annual Reports On-line. This free website provides access to British and foreign annual reports.

TELEPHONE AHEAD TO GATHER MORE INTELLIGENCE

Apart from the time, date and location of the interview, you will also need to know who you are going to be interviewed by. But there is other information that you should find out before your interview as well. Simply pick up the telephone and politely try to ask the recruitment coordinator, HR or the interviewer's secretary:

◆ How many people will be interviewing you?

◆ What are their names and job titles?

◆ Will there be just one interview or perhaps a series of interviews, or even some tests at an assessment centre?

◆ Do they have a job description for the vacancy? And will they let you see it beforehand?

Also try to sort out practical issues such as getting directions, or asking whether you will be able to claim for travel expenses. You do not want to bother the interviewer about such relatively trivial matters.

REHEARSE FOR THE BIG DAY

Role playing makes most people cringe – but it really is the single best method for sharpening up your interview technique. If you have a friend that you trust, then perhaps ask your friend to assume the role of the interviewer. Your friend could simply flick through Chapters 3 to 7 of this book to find appropriate questions to throw at you.

After the interview, you and your mock interviewer should go back over your answers to think about questions that you may have struggled with. Ideally, you would record your performance on videotape so that you could hear what you actually said as well as observe your body language during the mock interview. Recording yourself would also allow you to monitor whether you are speaking too quickly or slowly, quietly or loudly.

If you really cannot bring yourself to role play in front of a friend, then you could at least run through some of the questions and answers aloud. Perhaps standing in front of a mirror, flick to a random page in the middle of this book – again somewhere between Chapters 3 and 7 – read the question aloud and practise delivering a short, enthusiastic response.

SUMMARY

◆ Spend some time reflecting on what you think are your achievements, skills, strengths and weaknesses. What can you offer to an employer?

◆ Read and re-read the job advert to establish the questions you may be asked.

◆ Research some background around the organisation that you are going to be interviewed by. What can you bring to this particular employer to make them want to employ you?

◆ Sort out the logistics of the interview well before you have to turn up for the interview.

◆ Spend some time rehearsing.

2

Making the Right Impression

In this Chapter . . .

- ◆ Dressing appropriately
- ◆ Calming nerves
- ◆ Facing skilled and unskilled interviewers
- ◆ The importance of rapport
- ◆ Listening and responding carefully to questions
- ◆ Keeping it short and sweet

Many interviewers make up their minds about candidates in just the first few minutes of meeting them. How you look and behave in those first few minutes could make the instant difference between success and failure.

Put yourself into the interviewer's shoes for a moment. If you saw a scruffy-looking candidate in reception waiting to meet you, wouldn't you think that they were probably a bit disorganised in their work too? Or if a candidate were a bit nervous or stilted in introducing herself, wouldn't you suspect that she might be lacking in social skills with her colleagues as well?

So get your first impression right.

DON'T LET YOUR CLOTHES LET YOU DOWN

A book can't tell you exactly what to wear for every single interview. However, your friends might be able to give you some valuable advice on what to wear. So go ask your friends, colleagues and partner for their honest opinion. But if you ask them for advice, then be gracious enough to thank them for their advice and, above all, listen to their advice and incorporate some changes into your wardrobe.

The rules for men are simple:

- Wear a dark suit. Navy blue and grey are the most acceptable colours.
- Wear a long-sleeved shirt, either in white or a pale colour such as light blue.
- Choose an uncomplicated 100% silk tie. No one wears polyester anymore!
- Wear black shoes. Italians can get away with brown – but it just does not seem to work for the British!
- Allow yourself only three items of jewellery – a watch, a wedding ring and perhaps cuff links with a double-cuff shirt. Nothing more.

For women, the principles are not dissimilar:

- Also aim to wear a suit as opposed to separates.
- Wear a jacket and skirt as opposed to jacket and trousers. Unfortunately, some male interviewers can still be a bit sexist about skirts versus trousers.

- ◆ Choose a plain blouse. Don't try to look sexy – as your definition of sexy may be an interviewer's definition of tarty.
- ◆ Wear shoes that your grandmother would be happy with. High heels might be the height of fashion – but again some (typically older, male) interviewers may have negative views about them.
- ◆ Avoid unusual jewellery such as more than one earring per ear or thumb rings. Again you may get a negative reaction from older, male interviewers.

You may want to disagree with the rules. But there really is no point, as I didn't invent them – I'm just reporting them. So don't shoot the messenger! At the end of the day, you can wear what you like, but just be aware that there are some interviewers with quite traditional ideas about what is appropriate or not.

Dressing down

Increasingly, companies often have "smart casual" dress codes at work. However, be very, very careful if you are tempted to dress down to match the culture of a company. You may, for instance, find that an interviewer makes an effort to dress up in a suit when meeting candidates.

If you are planning to dress down, make sure you are 100% certain that this is the right move – perhaps if you have been told personally by the interviewer's secretary that he or she will be dressed casually. Far better to be overdressed than underdressed. A man, for example, could simply remove his tie and undo his top button to appear more relaxed – while women's suits tend to be suitable both in formal as well as smart-casual situations.

Avoiding blunders

Over the years, I have observed that some interviewers can attach a disproportionate amount of meaning to some relatively minor sartorial errors. So make sure that you:

- ◆ Polish your shoes. It is a cliché, but some interviewers can get a bit preoccupied when a candidate ruins a good suit by teaming it with scuffed shoes.
- ◆ Get a haircut a week before the interview. End of discussion.
- ◆ Check your personal hygiene – that means your breath and body odour. Ask your best friend in the world for an honest opinion. As an interviewer, I am frequently amazed by candidates who, for example, leave a trail of body odour in their wake or do not realise that they have bad breath. But neither is overly strong perfume or after-shave acceptable.

Pack a briefcase

You do not have to have a formal briefcase. However, it would help if you have a smart bag or case of some sort to carry with you:

- ◆ *Several copies of your CV or application form*. Occasionally, an interviewer may have been drafted in at the last minute and may not have your CV to hand.
- ◆ *A notepad and pen*. You may want to take notes – perhaps the most important facts about the company. Or when doing case study interviews (see Chapter 8), it may

help you with your calculations if you jot down a few of the key points.

◆ *Samples of any relevant work*. For example, if you are an architect or designer, you may want to bring along plans or diagrams to show the interviewer.

A touch of nerves can be a good thing

A dry mouth, racing pulse and sweaty palms – many candidates suffer a touch of anxiety before interviews. However, a modicum of tension can keep you alert and help you think more quickly on your feet.

Practice will help to dispel nervousness, but here are a few tips for reducing levels of anxiety on the day:

◆ **Slow your breathing right down**. Inhale to a count of four, hold your breath for a few counts, and then exhale to a count of four. Then repeat as necessary.

◆ **Imagine yourself being successful**. Visualise yourself walking into the interview, shaking hands with the interviewer, smiling, and then having a relaxed and confident discussion with the interviewer. Hold the image in your mind and paint as vivid a picture as you can. If you can make the scene vivid enough, you will be able to trick your body into thinking that it is reality.

◆ **Hold your hands under a cold tap**. Go to the bathroom and rinse your hands for a minute or so. When you have dried your hands, it will help you to avoid 'sweaty palm syndrome' – and it is a distracting activity that will reduce your anxiety levels. Failing that, discreetly keep your right hand wrapped around a handkerchief until you see an interviewer approaching to shake your hand.

NOT ALL INTERVIEWERS ARE SKILLED AT INTERVIEWING

There is a sliding scale of interviewer competence. At one end of the scale, you might be faced with a *skilled interviewer* who has been trained by the HR department to ask questions that will probe exactly what you have done in the past that would help their organisation to succeed. At the other extreme, you could be faced with an *unskilled interviewer* who may just have volunteered to interview for the first time because another colleague unexpectedly fell ill! The unskilled interviewer may not have any particular questions and may just be relying on gut feel to judge whether they can get on with you or not.

It is impossible to predict what sort of interviewer you will be faced with. You might think that more senior managers or interviewers in the larger, multinational or more sophisticated companies might be better trained than more junior managers or those in smaller organisations. But that is often not the case.

Giving examples

A skilled interviewer will ask probing questions about challenges you have faced, and may want examples along with detail as to what you did, why you did it, and what you learned. An unskilled interviewer may just ask some superficial questions.

But whether you are faced with a skilled or an unskilled interviewer, you should aim to *provide examples wherever possible* to back up your claims. Examples make a much stronger impact in the mind of the interviewer than generalised statements or opinions that you may make about yourself.

Consider the following exchange between an unskilled interviewer (I) and a candidate (C):

I: Are you a good team player?

C: Yes, I think I am.

I: Thank you. And now the next question . . .

However, compare it with an exchange in which the candidate gives a short example – even though the interviewer did not actually ask for one:

I: Are you a good team player?

C: Yes, I think I am. Just as one example, I have been taking part in a continuous improvement team for the last six months in addition to my day-to-day responsibilities. I have learnt a lot about working closely in a team to improve how we operate in the business. I can tell you much more about it if you like.

I: There's no need for now, but thank you. And now the next question . . .

As you can see, giving an example makes the candidate's response much more vivid – the candidate seems more believable in professing to have good team skills. A skilled interviewer will automatically ask for examples, but an unskilled interviewer may forget to do so. So try to give an example to substantiate your claims and make yourself more memorable.

FOCUS ON RAPPORT AS WELL AS THE INTERVIEW QUESTIONS

How you respond to questions is just as important as what you say. After all, an interviewer is trying to answer two questions to his or her satisfaction during an interview:

1. Can you, the candidate, do the job?
2. Would he or she *enjoy* working with you?

Interpersonal chemistry is very important in interviews – many interviewers are more interested in selecting a candidate that they like than one who has the right skills. After all, would you want to work with someone who was technically very good at the job, but rather boring or unbearably arrogant? You need to make the interviewer not only think highly of your skills but also *want* to work with you.

The Pittsburgh Airport test

When I worked for a large American management consulting firm, there used to be an anecdote about the kind of candidates we wanted to recruit. Of course we wanted to identify bright, committed individuals. But we also wanted them to be able to pass the 'Pittsburgh Airport test'.

Put yourself in the following situation. A transferring flight has stopped at Pittsburgh Airport. Your connecting flight has been cancelled and your next flight will now not leave for 24 hours. If you were stuck with the person you are interviewing, how would you feel about it?

As interviewers, we were asked to think about whether we could spend 24 hours with each candidate we interviewed. So skills and experience sometimes do not matter if you don't come across as someone with whom people could *enjoy* spending time.

First contact

The first few minutes of most interviews are choreographed as if they were a dance. When meeting your interviewer for the first time, try to:

◆ Make eye contact and smile broadly.
◆ Shake hands firmly – but without crushing your interviewer's hand.
◆ Make a few minutes of polite conversation or 'chit-chat' while the interviewer is leading you to the room that will be used for the interview. If the interviewer does not initiate any conversation, you could always fill the silence by making a few comments on the 'lovely offices' or perhaps some small piece of (good) news that you have recently heard about the company or the industry in general. But follow the interviewer's lead – while certain interviewers genuinely enjoy making small talk, others may want to press on almost immediately with interview questions.
◆ Wait to be invited to take a seat.

Conventions of rapport building

Rapport is not established at any particular point in the interview. Working on building rapport is something that you need to do throughout the interview:

◆ Maintain **eye contact** throughout the interview. Research tells us that you should look your interviewer in the eyes when he or she is speaking. However, it is acceptable to glance away when it is your turn to speak, for example many people look at some spot in the middle distance when pausing for a moment to construct an appropriate response to an interview question.

◆ **Nod** in agreement whenever the interviewer says something that you agree with.

◆ Allow your personality to shine through. **Smile** and, if appropriate, even show that you have a sense of humour.

If the idea of rapport seems baffling, a good exercise is to look around you at the people you work with. The next time you are in a meeting, watch your colleagues and ask yourself who looks bored? Who looks motivated and fired up? And then analyse what it is that they say, how they say it, and how their faces, hands and bodies move to give off a good or bad impression.

Another method that some candidates swear by is to **match your speech patterns and body language with those of your interviewer**. For example, if your interviewer is speaking very slowly and ponderously, you should respond slowly. Or if your interviewer remains almost motionless throughout the interview, then you should as well.

More body language

Learn to monitor the signals that your body is sending during interviews. If you reply to the questions in the right way, a skilled interviewer will probably give you the job. However, the problem comes when you are faced by an unskilled interviewer who may simply become fixated by some minor tic or trait of yours.

Typical lapses to look out for include:

◆ Making wild gestures with your hands.
◆ Fidgeting with your hands or playing with a pen, ring, cuff links etc.
◆ Tensing up your shoulders.
◆ Speaking too quickly. If you feel yourself becoming nervous, try swallowing between sentences – this forces you to slow down.
◆ Biting or chewing your lips.
◆ Crossing and uncrossing your legs frequently.

If you are worried about your body language, ask your colleagues or close friends whether you have any particular mannerisms when you are nervous. On the other hand, do not become obsessed with your body language. So long as you can smile, speak slowly and answer the questions well, you're 90% of the way home.

LISTEN AND RESPOND TO THE QUESTION THAT IS BEING ASKED

Candidates can sometimes annoy the interviewer by answering the question they *think* was asked, rather than the one that was *actually* asked. The situation is not helped by the fact that unskilled interviewers can sometimes (inadvertently or occasionally deliberately) ask questions that are convoluted and difficult to answer.

In order to make sure that this does not happen to you:

◆ Listen to the entire question that is being asked rather than just plucking out the key words or trying to predict the question that you think the interviewer may ask. For example, you might hear the phrase 'greatest achievement' and be ready to recount a description of a recent success at work – but the interviewer may have been asking: 'What is your greatest achievement outside of work?'

◆ Don't ignore parts of a question that you may not want to answer. For example, when I ask candidates, "What are your strengths and weaknesses?" it irritates me when they talk about their strengths, and try to get away without revealing any weaknesses.

◆ Ask for clarification if you are not 100% sure of the question. "Sorry, I'm not sure I understand, could you repeat the question please?"

BE CONCISE IN YOUR RESPONSES

Interviewers try their best to listen to candidates. But they are only human too. And when they come to interview you, they may already have met several other candidates and been bored by at least one or two of them.

So when an interviewer asks you a simple question, keep your answers short to begin with. Then, if you think that the interviewer might like to hear more, you could ask, "shall I go on?" or "would you like an example of that?" before giving more detail to back up your initial response.

A good analogy is to think of your answers as icebergs. Your first answer might be the tip of the iceberg. But if the interviewer does not understand what you mean or is interested by what you are saying, then you should give them the opportunity to listen to the rest of the story – delving into the bulk of the iceberg that is hidden from view.

What follows in Chapters 3 through to 7 are examples of the many questions that you could get asked by interviewers. These hundred or so questions should cover almost anything that an interviewer could throw at you. Read the advice and sample answers. **But you must think about your own experiences and come up with an answer to each question that is relevant to you**. You need to find words that you feel comfortable with, and it is much easier to be convincing if you are being honest. If you try to learn the sample answers parrot-fashion, an interviewer will very quickly see through you. You have been warned!

SUMMARY

- ◆ Dress conservatively and take advice from a trusted friend on how you look.

- ◆ Keep excessive nervousness at bay by distracting yourself and engaging in positive thinking exercises.

- ◆ Understand that skilled and unskilled interviewers may have very different strategies but in either case give examples of when you have used key skills.

◆ Remember that interviewers are not just looking for the most efficient or effective candidate, but also the one that they like and could have a drink with.

◆ Listen carefully and check that you understand all of the parts of a question before plunging into an answer.

◆ Answer questions briefly and check that the interviewer wants you to go on.

◆ Ensure your responses are your own and not learnt by heart from a book or 'borrowed' from someone else.

3

Dealing with Standard Questions

In this Chapter . . .

◆ What are the basic questions you must be ready for?
◆ Answering questions about your career history
◆ Thinking about your future career
◆ Responding to questions about time
◆ Impressing with your technical knowledge

There are certain questions that the vast majority of interviewers like to use. Interviewers want to know about the decisions you have taken to get you where you are in your career, why you are looking for a new job, and why you believe you should work for them.

But whatever question is asked in the end, remember to *provide examples whenever possible*. Claims are nothing if they are not substantiated. Examples make a much stronger impact in the mind of the interviewer than generalised statements or opinions that you may make about yourself.

ALMOST ALL INTERVIEWERS WILL ASK SOME OF THESE QUESTIONS

Read through the questions and the advice – then write down a few notes on how you would respond to each question.

So, tell me about yourself

Many interviewers like to begin by asking this question. The open-ended nature of the question means that you could potentially answer it in any number of ways. So start by checking how much information the interviewer wants: "Is there any part of my CV that you would like me to focus on?" The interviewer's response should hopefully direct you to the areas that he or she is most interested in.

Even if the interviewer does not give you any further guidance, you should avoid talking about your family, hobbies and interests outside of work, or goals in life. After all, if you want to convince the interviewer that you are the right person for the job, you should focus on the skills that are needed to fill the vacancy – unless the interviewer specifically asks you to talk about any of those areas.

To prepare for this question, look at the job advert. What skills and qualities does the advert talk about? If it says that they are looking for 'a head teacher with excellent planning and problem solving skills', then be prepared to talk about your planning and problem solving skills in your initial response.

As an example, consider the following excerpt from a job advert:

> *Growing London-based accountancy firm is looking to open a regional office in Birmingham. We are looking for an office manager to set up an office and recruit a team of secretarial staff to support eight accountants.*

A candidate might then respond along the lines of the following: "As you can see from my CV, I have six years' experience of office management from two companies – the most recent of which has been for a law firm, so I have plenty of experience working for demanding and highly motivated professional services staff. In my current job, I look after all of the office functions – from the computer, photocopying and telephone systems, to managing a team of three secretaries to ensure that the solicitors get the support that they need. Shall I go on?"

What does your day-to-day job involve?

Rather than giving a blow-by-blow account of what you do in a typical day, you should be selective in your response. Try to include in your answer the sorts of tasks that you would be doing if you were to be offered the job.

The office manager from the previous question might reply by saying: "I start the day by speaking in person with all of the professional staff to check what their requirements for the day might be. Then I hold a brief meeting with my team to ensure that no one has a huge workload while someone else isn't very busy. Further than that, it's very hard to say exactly what else I might be doing – as I try to be responsive to the needs of the professional staff, as well as any issues in my team."

What do you like/enjoy in your work? What do you most like about your job?

Your tactic for responding to this question should be very similar to that for dealing with the previous question about your day-to-day job. Again, think about the main responsibilities – such as meeting prospective customers, writing proposals, and presenting at meetings – in the job that you are being interviewed for. Then incorporate these into your reply.

What motivates you?

Ideally, you should be able to tell the interviewer that you are most motivated when you are helping the organisation to achieve its goals. If, for example, you were being interviewed by an aggressive American investment bank, they might like to hear you talk about your financial motivations: "I get a real kick out of negotiating good deals with clients that will bring revenue into the company and make me a wealthy person in the process." Then proceed to give a concrete example of when you have negotiated a good deal.

Or if you were being interviewed by a not-for-profit organisation: "I like to know that my work is making a difference." Again, continue by giving an example of when you have done something worthwhile.

If you are not sure about the organisation's goals, you could always reply by mentioning one of the following:

- A thirst for knowledge – "I really enjoy picking up new skills and I don't mind working hard so long as I am developing myself."
- Teamwork – "I am most motivated when I am surrounded by bright people who also have a desire to get things done."
- Problem solving – "I like solving problems. When faced with a problem, I like working out options, weighing up the pros and cons of alternatives, and then sorting it out."

Again, in each instance, continue by giving an example of when you have picked up new skills, worked in a team, etc.

What frustrates you about your current job? What do you most dislike about your work?

An interviewer will not believe you if you say that you enjoy every single moment of your job. A good trick is to talk about inefficient systems, unwieldy processes or bureaucracy. However, when you do give your example, either allude to the fact that it is entirely out of your control or that you have tried to improve the situation but have good reasons for not being able to change it. It would be even better if you can say that the situation is currently being fixed due to your efforts.

For example: "I spend most of my time visiting clients at their offices. However, it continually irritates me that we don't have the facility to log on to the server remotely from our laptop computers. I have tried to convince the IT manager that we need to upgrade our system, but he says that we won't have the budget until next year."

Or talk about minor aspects of the work that do not affect your ability to do the job. "The paperwork can be very time-consuming, but I realise that it's a necessary evil. I've learnt to just lock myself in my office for half a day a week to get it out of the way."

How would you describe your current company?

Some interviewers have it in their minds that a candidate that knocks a current or previous employer could be a troublemaker. It may not be fair or right – but if you want the job, you should ideally be able to give the impression that you enjoy working at your current company, but that there are just one or two aspects of your interviewer's organisation that are even more attractive.

As an example: "The people are great – they are very talented and committed to doing good work. However, it's such a large international business that I don't feel that I make a difference – that's why I'm looking to join a smaller company where I can more quickly work my way up to becoming a partner."

What do you know about this company?

This question should never be a problem if you have done your research (see Chapter 1). Your aim in answering the question should be to show that you have done some reading or speaking to colleagues, then finish by providing a short example of a skill or some aspect of your previous experience that ties in to the organisation's needs.

"My understanding from speaking to people in the industry is that your company is experiencing a squeeze on profit margins due to increased competition from aggressive American entrants into the market. However, I have experience of having grown sales and profits in my current job by over 20% for three years running, so I am confident that I would be able to make a contribution to the business."

What have you done recently to develop yourself?

Employers value employees who continually look to improve themselves. Two of the best answers include:

◆ A course that you are taking, for example: "I've just started an MBA with the Open University. It will take me two years, but I want to improve my financial skills and expand my network of business contacts."

◆ A project that is expanding your skills. You could say: "I recently volunteered to work as part of a new product development team. We are interviewing customers and suppliers to figure out what other products we could be manufacturing, so I am getting a lot of exposure to customers that I wouldn't normally meet in my day-to-day role in the back office."

If you are struggling to talk about a course or project, you could probably mention a book that you are reading to improve your skills or understanding at work. "I've just started reading a book about 'Total Quality Management', which I hope will help me to boost productivity in the team."

Or perhaps talk about an endeavour outside of work that will improve a skill at work. For example: "I'm currently spending one Saturday a month working with a support group for the long-term unemployed. It is giving me a great deal of exposure to people with different backgrounds, which I hope will help me to understand and manage my team more effectively too."

What kind of salary are you after?

Avoid talking about this in a first interview, as you don't want to price yourself out of the market. Nor do you want to mention a salary that is far lower than what they might be willing to pay.

A good answer might be: "I'm looking for a challenging role that will give me the opportunity to work on new projects, so the salary is only part of what I'm looking for." If you were feeling brave you might throw the question back at the interviewer: "What kind of salary range would you be looking to give someone for this role?"

However, if the interviewer persists and asks you a second time, you may need to give them a rough idea – but again, without pricing yourself out of the market. Try something along the lines of, "I'd be looking for in the region of £28,000 to £35,000 but, as I said, the exact package is less important to me than finding a challenging job role. So I'd rather hold off on giving you an exact figure until I find out more about the role."

There is more advice on how to negotiate salary in Chapter 12.

What do you do outside of work?

Again, you need to have done your research on the employer to gauge the sorts of things that you might want to talk about. For example, if their website says that they possess a ''work hard, play hard'' culture, you might say: ''Quite a few of my colleagues at work are also my friends outside of work. So we like to have the occasional drink/ meal out/game of football together.''

Be careful what you talk about. Mentioning activities to do with your faith or religion has been known (unfortunately) to turn some interviewers off. Talking about your family excessively may also give the interviewer the impression that you may not be willing to work long hours when necessary.

Do you play any competitive sports?

Some interviewers believe that candidates who play team sports are also more likely to be good team players in the workplace. But even if you do not play a team sport, it is still better to talk about some form of exercise that you engage in, rather than nothing at all. Some interviewers are suspicious of couch potatoes.

Do you have any problems with relocating?

If relocation is necessary for the job, you should have already picked this up in your research. However, if the question comes as a complete shock to you in the interview, a good response that allows you to play for time might be: ''I didn't realise that relocation would be required for this job, but I have to say that I am very keen to join the company, from what I have seen and heard about the company so far. So, depending on the right package, relocation would not be a problem.''

May we approach your referees?

It is natural to be concerned about having your references checked if your current employer does not know that you are looking for a job. "I'd be happy for you to check my references eventually, but could I please ask you to hold off for the moment? My employer doesn't know that I am currently looking for a job, so I'd rather wait until I had a firm job offer on the table before alerting them."

If you wanted to hammer home your best points, you could finish off by telling the interviewer what you think your references might say: "However, I know that my boss would tell you that . . ." and so on.

BE READY TO EXPLAIN ABOUT THE DIRECTION OF YOUR CAREER

Interviewers are frequently interested to hear about the decisions that you have made in your career. Why did you take a certain job? And why *didn't* you take certain jobs?

Talk me through your career

First, find out how far back in your career the interviewer would like you to go: "Would you like me to start from when I left school, or would you like me to focus on the years since I completed my MBA?"

In any case, this is not an invitation to ramble at length about your career. Instead, think about how you can summarise why you left or joined each company that you have worked for.

"I must be honest – I didn't have a grand plan when I left school, so my father suggested I take an engineering apprenticeship with Ultro, a local firm. I was very quickly promoted to be a team supervisor. After five good years, I felt that I had learnt everything that I could there, so I moved to Factory Magix, which was a much bigger company. Then, three years ago, I had the opportunity to move sideways into the marketing team to do something completely different."

Then finish off with your reasons for looking for a new job. "I've now discovered that I really enjoy marketing – but Factory Magix has only a small marketing department, which brings me to this interview with you."

Have you ever regretted anything about your career?

"Regret" is a strong word – so it is best to avoid confessing that you have had any serious regrets. If you must make an admission, try to talk about a decision that happened a long time ago that could in no way reflect badly on you in this interview. "I don't regret the course of my career, because I have worked in some interesting companies and succeeded in my chosen profession. However, I do sometimes wish that I had taken an overseas secondment while I was working with Medical Logistics back in the 80s when I was young, free and single, to have had the experience of immersing myself in another culture."

Why are you looking for another job?

Three of the best reasons to cite are:

◆ More challenge – "I've enjoyed my years with the company. But in recent months I have begun to feel bored, so I'm looking for new challenges to keep me interested in my work."

◆ Greater security – "The directors didn't manage the business very well, so we were always on the verge of a cash flow crisis. I don't like having to worry about my job, so I'm looking to join a more successful company."

◆ Better rewards – "I know that I can make a significant contribution to my employer, so rather than just earning a salary, I would like to be able to take an equity stake in a growing business."

Try to avoid saying that you left a previous employer due to any sort of personal conflict. For example, that you did not get on with your boss, or that the company failed to give you the promotion that you wanted. Such comments could reflect badly on you – the interviewer may start to wonder whether you were in part to blame for not getting on with your boss or not being offered a promotion.

Why do you want to leave your current employer?

This is just a variation of the last question. Again, just remember to emphasise the positive qualities of the interviewing organisation as opposed to whingeing about negative aspects of your current employment situation. For example, mentioning that your current commuting time is too long makes you sound like a moaner – so try to talk about something else.

How would you describe your ideal job?

Don't fall into the trap of talking about what you would expect from an employer – such as the salary and benefits. Instead, talk about what you could contribute to the organisation. For instance: "I enjoy passing on my expertise to the people around me. I know that I can only move upwards in my career by developing the people in my team to be my successor."

Why do you want this job in particular?

Think about how the organisation likes to present itself to the outside world. How does this one company believe it is different from its competitors? Select a few of these unique characteristics about the organisation and incorporate them into your reply.

Many companies, for instance, believe themselves to have a good reputation or to be leaders in their field. "You have an excellent reputation in the marketplace. Even compared with other firms such as Young Samson & Chalmers, I think that you are recognised by your clients as being truly leading edge."

Or the organisation may think that its employees are a breed apart from the rest. "I've been impressed by the quality of thinking of all of the employees that I have met so far."

How does this job compare with other jobs you are applying for?

In the past, interviewers could get a bit uppity when candidates admitted to having applied to more than just their company. However, in today's more mobile economy, most employers recognise that good candidates do shop around.

A bit of flattery about the company that is interviewing you would not go amiss – just don't overdo it. "I have to say that the people at the other firms were also very bright. But I also have to say that, even though this is obviously only my second interview with you, I prefer what I have heard so far about your incentive scheme."

Would you rather be a big fish in a small pond or a small fish in a big pond?

The employer wants to know whether you would rather work for a small company or a large employer. Think about what might be relevant to this particular employer.

The benefits of working in a smaller company might include:

◆ A greater sense of ownership in your work.
◆ Being able to see that you are making a visible contribution to the bottom line.
◆ Greater exposure to – and therefore opportunities to learn from – senior management.
◆ A chance to take an equity stake at an earlier stage in your career.

The benefits of working for a larger company could include:

◆ A better company brand that will look good on your CV.
◆ Better access to structured training programmes.

◆ Opportunities to work in offices elsewhere – perhaps even internationally.

◆ More financial stability and security.

BE READY TO TALK ABOUT YOUR FUTURE CAREER DIRECTION

Employee turnover costs organisations money. If they decide to offer you the job, they would like to know that their investment in training you and getting you up to speed would be repaid by a good stint working for them.

Where do you see yourself in five years' time?

Ah, 'that old chestnut'. If most candidates were honest, they would be forced to admit that they actually have no career plan. Unfortunately, interviewers like to hear that you have thought about the future.

If the interviewer could be your future boss, it might be dangerous to say that you would like their job. However, it is increasingly acceptable for you to say that you might be ready for the next step in your career. Most employers would feel that they had got a return on their investment if you stayed for five years.

A personnel administrator applying for a job as a manager might say: "I would hope to have completed my IPD exams and be on my way towards finding a role as a Personnel Director."

What would you consider a reasonable length of time to stay in a job?

A good response might be to separate out the length of time you would stay in a *job* as opposed to the time you would stay with the *company*.

"I believe that it would only take me between two to four years to master this role. Once I have learnt everything I can about the job, I would be looking to move into a bigger role with greater responsibilities. However, I would hope that there would be other opportunities in the company without the need to look externally."

What do you think you should be earning in three years' time?

You need to be careful that your ambitions match the ability of the company to provide you with raises in your salary. Just as an example, a librarian in a public sector organisation is less likely to be able to double their salary than a barrister in the same period.

So make sure that your response takes into account what you understand the market would pay for someone with three more years of experience than yourself. You could try answering the question briefly and moving quickly on: "I hope that my pay will reflect my contribution to the organisation, but the most important thing for me is having a variety of different projects to work on that will keep me employable."

Do you have any personal goals that you have yet to achieve?

Even though the question asks you about personal goals, it is always safer to talk about a goal that would make you more valuable to your employer. Accordingly, you might want to talk about how you would develop a new skill by getting involved in projects that take you out of your 'comfort zone'. Courses and vocational qualifications are also good answers here.

INTERVIEWERS CAN WORRY ABOUT TOO SHORT OR TOO LONG A TIME WITH A COMPANY

Frequent job changes in your past could imply that you are a difficult employee. However, employers can also worry about you being too long with just one company – as they may be concerned that you will not be able to cope with the transition to a new working environment.

You seem to have changed jobs very frequently. Why is that?

Employers can worry that you will join and get trained up, only to move on again. So you must be ready to give a good reason for each and every one of your job moves. For example, you may have genuinely completed what you set out to do in that company – such as learning a particular skill, or turning around a team before moving on to a new challenge.

Or, there may have been a common reason for having changed jobs several times, such as:

◆ Previous family circumstances – "My husband's job at the time meant that we had to relocate a couple of times, which was quite disruptive to my own career. But my husband has since joined a company where he doesn't have to travel at all, so now I'm keen to join a company where I can get settled."

◆ Youth – "It's true that I have dabbled in a variety of jobs, but that was early on in my career, just after I had graduated. But I think I have now sorted in my own mind what I want out of my career."

You seem to have stayed in your role/company for a long time. Why is that?

If you have been with one company but taken on a variety of different roles, explain that each role has given you new challenges and that you saw no reason to leave – until now. Effectively, you should be able to argue that you genuinely had, for example, ten years of experience as opposed to one year of experience repeated ten times. Then continue with your reasons for wanting to work with this new employer.

It is trickier if you have been in just the one job for a long time without having been promoted. Perhaps your reasons are to do with your family: "I didn't want to take on a managerial role because I wanted to have an active role in bringing up our two young children. But now that they are at secondary school, I'm ready to get my career back on track by taking on new responsibilities."

Given you have stayed in your company for a long time, how will you cope with a new one?

The interviewer is expressing a concern that you may

struggle to make the transition to a new environment with fresh faces and different ways of working. Put the interviewer's fears to rest by providing an example of how you have made some sort of successful transition at work.

"I've had to deal with a lot of change in my time at this company. Only six months ago, my company made 20% of our team redundant to reduce costs. However, I was chosen to work with HR to restructure the team. Even though it was an uncomfortable situation for a while, I not only adapted to it, but also helped others to adjust to it too."

BE READY FOR QUESTIONS ABOUT YOUR TECHNICAL AREA

Your CV may look good, but employers can still wonder whether you have the technical expertise to do the job. An IT consultant may get asked about hardware options and software applications. A university lecturer could be asked to discuss two opposing theories in his or her subject area. An HR officer might get asked questions about European employee legislation and disciplinary procedures.

So what are the key technical questions that you might be asked?

Make sure that you will not get caught out. Take 20 minutes and a blank sheet of paper to list the 20 or so most likely questions that you might be asked. If you discover that you have any gaps in your knowledge, now is a good time to go do some reading and find out the answer.

SUMMARY

◆ Read through the questions in this chapter and think about how you would respond to each of them.

◆ Tailor your answers so that what you say ties in exactly with the skills that the employer is looking for.

◆ Be ready to talk about the reasons behind each of the career decisions that you have ever made.

◆ Be prepared to talk about your career future too.

◆ Think about technical questions that you might be asked – as no book will ever be able to give you these on a plate.

$$\boxed{4}$$

Responding to Competency-Based Questions

In this Chapter . . .

◆ What are competencies?
◆ Understanding the layers beneath competency-based questions
◆ A sample question and full response
◆ Questions about achievement and self-motivation
◆ Questions about conflict and difficult people
◆ Questions that focus on problem solving and judgement

Increasingly, employers are using 'competency-based' (also sometimes called 'behavioural' or 'situational') interviewing techniques to separate out the good candidates from those who are simply trying to bluff their way into the job without the right skills or experience.

Competencies are simply an elaborate term often used by organisations to describe 'behaviours that are linked to success at work' – in other words, competencies are the key skills that the interviewer is looking for. Many organisations have spent time thinking about the skills that they want all of their employees to have. Whatever the exact duties of your job, whether you are applying to be a social worker, an auditor or airline cabin crew – employers will almost always be looking for people who are self-motivated, can solve problems, and have good people skills.

COMPETENCY-BASED QUESTIONS LOOK AT PREVIOUS EXAMPLES OF REAL BEHAVIOUR

The theory behind competency-based interviewing is that past work behaviour is a good predictor of future job performance. When interviewers ask you competency-based questions, *they want you to talk about how you have actually tackled real problems in the past*. From this, they are trying to infer how effectively you would tackle future problems if they were to offer you a job.

This style of questioning differs from asking you to talk about how you generally go about confronting issues or how you might deal with hypothetical scenarios. The interviewers want you to think about actual situations that you have faced. As such, competency-based questions are fairly easy to spot. They start off with verbal phrases like:

◆ "Give me an example of . . ."
◆ "Can you think of an occasion when you have . . . ?"
◆ "Tell me about a situation where you . . ."
◆ "Describe an instance when . . ."

In responding to a competency-based question, the most important principle is to: **Give a real example that actually**

happened to you. Don't talk in broad terms about how you generally tackle those sorts of situations. Talk about a specific example.

Once you have talked about your example, the interviewer will probably ask you further questions to get a deeper understanding of what you did. So, the second key principle is: **Be ready to talk about your example in a lot of detail**.

COMPETENCY-BASED QUESTIONS ARE DESIGNED TO CATCH OUT LIARS

Competency-based questions help interviewers to catch out candidates who have exaggerated their skills or experience. A candidate who is trying to bluff their way into the job will be comfortable talking about their experience only at a high level and not in any detail. So a skilled competency-based interviewer will ask for a lot of detail around each question.

Just imagine yourself in the following scenario for a moment. You are a police officer and have just arrested a suspect that you think burgled a house at 9.35pm on Friday 15 July. Your first question might be: "Where were you at 9.35pm on Friday 15 July?" – to which the suspect replies that he was "alone at home, watching television". In order to catch him out, you might want to ask further questions such as: "What were you watching?" To which the suspect might say that he was watching his favourite soap opera. Again, to try to uncover his lying, you might ask: "So what was happening in that particular episode?"

Now think of the interviewer as a police officer – and you, the candidate, as a suspect. The interviewer is trying to uncover whether you really used a particular skill or not. Interview candidates who are overstating their experience will not have the background information or be able to talk about their experience in detail. However, **good candidates will be able to talk about their experiences in depth**.

Your aim is to provide a 'fly on the wall' experience for the interviewer so that they can almost imagine themselves having been there when your experience happened.

AN EXAMPLE OF A QUESTION AND DETAILED RESPONSE

Imagine that an interviewer has asked a candidate the following question: "Please describe to me a situation when you have helped a colleague who was in trouble. What was the situation and how did you try to tackle it?"

On the face of it, it seems a fairly straightforward question to answer. However, a crafty interviewer could interrupt you at any point and follow up with all sorts of supplementary questions. Look at the following sample candidate's response. You will see certain underlined words and phrases, which indicate points at which the interviewer might want to interrupt to ask for further information.

The candidate's response might go along the lines of the following: "There was a time when James, the sales manager, came to me with a problem about his sales performance. He asked for some advice, so I tried to be supportive and make some suggestions. I also helped him on some <u>site visits</u> to customers. And, over the course of the next few months, he listened to my advice and managed to bring his performance up to satisfactory levels again."

So, supplementary questions (along with the candidate's responses) could include:

- <u>Time</u> – "How recently did this happen?" The candidate responds: "This was three years ago, when I'd just moved from the sales department to being the marketing manager. When I left the sales department, they recruited a young sales manager to take over my old role."
- <u>Came to me</u> – "Why did he come to you?" The candidate responds: "He came to me because we'd already struck up a good working relationship by that point. It was a small company, so I always tried to meet with new colleagues and take them out for a drink and explain to them that I was there if they ever needed any help."
- <u>Problem</u> – "And what was the sales manager's problem?" The candidate explains: "James wasn't hitting his sales targets. James was a really bright person – but didn't have that much sales experience."
- <u>Sales performance</u> – "What exactly was wrong with his performance?" The candidate replies: "James had two major targets. His first target was that he had to cold call enough companies every month to set up five meetings with prospective clients. His other target was to convert 50% of prospective clients into real customers. He was failing on both of them."
- <u>Supportive</u> – "How were you supportive?" The candidate explains: "James was on the verge of tears and

really agitated about his poor performance because he was worried he was going to get fired. The first thing I did was to get him to calm down. I took him out of the office and bought him a coffee and tried to listen to him without judging him."

◆ <u>Suggestions</u> – "So what were your suggestions?" The candidate responds: "After talking to him and understanding that he was failing to meet both of his targets, my first suggestion was that I might listen in on some of his cold calls. So I spent a few hours one morning listening in on his cold calls. I discovered that he was telephoning customers without first doing enough research on them. He called them up without knowing anything about their business needs. So I worked with James to think about the sorts of facts that he would need to collect before making a call.'

◆ <u>Site visits</u> – "Tell me a bit more about what you did on these site visits." The candidate responds: "I also talked James round to letting me attend a couple of sales meetings with him. I went along, observed him and gave him some constructive comments about what he was doing wrong. In particular, he was being a bit too aggressive in trying to get the customer to sign on the dotted line there and then. So I persuaded him to give customers more thinking time – which resulted in more of them signing up in the end."

As you can see, a candidate who did not actually experience that situation would have found it difficult to provide so much detail. From the initial question then, the interviewer could have asked any number of supplementary questions – all of which you would need to have good answers to.

Preparing yourself

Now that you understand the sorts of questions that an interviewer could ask you, you should recognise the need to prepare your responses in some detail before an interview. In order to equip yourself to respond well to any competency-based questions, you should:

◆ Look at the job advert (and job description if you have one). What key skills do they list for the job? Also, what key skills are not mentioned, but implied for the job?
◆ Think of likely questions that an interviewer could ask you about each competency. Don't forget to think about technical skills – such as being able to find legal cases quickly for solicitors or being able to identify errors in computer code for computer programmers.
◆ Think of an example of when you have used that skill.
◆ And then think of a second example of when you have used that skill. Interviewers often ask two very similar questions to weed out ill-equipped from well-prepared candidates.
◆ Finally, think about the follow-on questions that the interviewer might ask you – and how would you answer each one of those supplementary questions?

THINK ABOUT HOW YOU HAVE MOTIVATED YOURSELF TO ACHIEVE RESULTS

Employers look for candidates who are self-motivated and driven to succeed. But they also want candidates who can actually achieve something and make a difference.

What is your biggest achievement? Why is it an achievement and what did you do?

This question could be answered in any number of ways, but try to keep your response specific to the job. You should be as specific as possible about the benefits that you achieved – these could include:

◆ Increased profit or market share.
◆ Saved time or reduced costs.
◆ Better relationships with customers, clients, suppliers, or other stakeholders.
◆ Improved morale of colleagues.

For example: "I was proudest of the time that I assembled a committee to examine how we deal with patients at the surgery. We identified that many patients were waiting longer than necessary to get appointments because our administrators were processing the paperwork manually. After inviting colleagues from the IT and admin depart-ments, we made a recommendation to the trustees that we should put in a new computer system. We delivered the system on time and on budget, with the result that we cut waiting times from 18 days to ten days."

As in the above example, try to keep your initial answer fairly brief. The interviewer will prompt you by asking you further questions for more detail. Likely follow-up questions include:

◆ "Why is it your biggest achievement?"
◆ "Who first identified the problem or situation?"

◆ "What was your specific role on the team – as opposed to what your colleagues did?"

◆ "What problems or obstacles did you experience along the way? And how did you resolve these?"

◆ "What did you learn from this experience?"

If your biggest achievement happened three years ago, why have you not achieved anything else since then?

A tough question, but do not let it throw you. Parry the question by saying: "That was an achievement of which I was especially proud of, but I have accomplished other things since then. For example . . ." Then go on to talk about another achievement.

What is your second/third/etc biggest achievement?

Be ready to talk about a number of different achievements. Most candidates will have thought about their main achievement – but only the best candidates will be ready to talk about more than one achievement. This is your opportunity to shine!

What is the greatest challenge you have faced? How did you respond to the challenge?

The interviewer is trying to see how you cope with adversity. Again, steer clear of personal challenges – such as balancing childcare against work commitments or a personal tragedy such as bereavement. While these may actually be your greatest challenges and have helped to mould you into the person that you are, remember that the interviewer is looking for someone who can overcome the sorts of challenges that you would face in the workplace.

In answering this question, think back to an occasion when you were faced with a problem that seemed insurmountable. Perhaps it was a task that your colleagues said could not be done. Maybe no one else had ever done it this way before. And then, when talking about how you tackled the problem and triumphed, try to emphasise your personal contribution as opposed to what the rest of the team did.

How have you planned and organised for a big project?

A good plan is of no use if it does not come off or you end up dramatically overspending – so employers look for organising skills, as well as being able to deliver plans on time and within an agreed budget.

If you worked as part of a team, be ready to talk about how you allocated roles and responsibilities – how did you decide who should do what?

Supplementary questions to prepare for include:

- "To what extent did you make contingencies in the plan?"
- "How did you measure progress along the way?"
- "Did progress slip against the plan at any point? If so, what did you do to get it back on track again?"
- "What were the biggest obstacles that you faced along the way? How did you tackle these?"
- "What have you learned from this experience? What would you do differently next time?"

Have you ever failed in anything?

Again, keep your response focused on the workplace – avoid

talking about setbacks such as the breakdown of a significant relationship in your life, or failure to achieve a personal goal.

Given that this is a negatively phrased question, the way to respond well is by showing that you learnt something from the experience that you can apply in the future. Or, talk about an occasion when your efforts would have succeeded – were it not for unforeseen circumstances that were completely out of your control.

Describe a mistake that you made at work and what you did after you identified the mistake

Everyone makes mistakes – so if you claim never to have made a mistake, the interviewer will just think that you are being defensive. However, don't spend too long spelling out the mistake when the interviewer is most interested in the action you took to rectify it. Try also to highlight what you learned from the experience.

For example: "I worked in the IT support department for a small company. A couple of the team had been sick so I got some temporary staff in. I asked one of the temps to install new virus protection software on all of the company's laptops. It wasn't until about a month later that I discovered that he hadn't finished the job. A virus that stopped everyone from printing affected about 30 of the laptops. So I had to go around each person's laptop, removing the virus and installing the protection software. It took me about two hours to do each one and I worked until past midnight for four days in a row to get it all done. I don't blame the temp – it was my fault I hadn't checked that he'd had time to complete the installation. But I learned the hard way not to assume work has been completed without checking it personally."

Can you provide me with an example of how you have demonstrated initiative?

This is an opportunity for you to talk about an activity or project that you started on your own – without prompting or being told to do so by someone else.

For example: "The charity I worked for used to run almost entirely on donations from the public collected by our volunteers rattling collecting tins, but donations were falling by over 10% per year. We identified that it would only be two years before we would be forced to close the animal shelter. My colleagues saw this as simply inevitable, but I was determined not to let it happen. So I just picked up the local telephone directory and spent two weeks phoning up local businesses to try to get their support. I called over 300 companies and got turned down by 99% of them. But I managed to persuade nine local businesses to donate £11,000 in return for allowing them to put our logo on their corporate Christmas cards. As such, we identified that the charity does have a future – but that we need to collect from corporate sponsors in the future, rather than the general public."

THINK ABOUT HOW YOU HAVE HANDLED DIFFICULT PEOPLE

Almost all employers are interested in whether you have 'people skills' or not. They want to explore the extent to which you can influence, persuade, or motivate others to achieve results on your behalf.

Who is the most difficult person you have ever worked with? Why was that person difficult? What did you try to do about it?

This question is trying to determine how you deal with conflict. Try to avoid talking about any anger or emotion that you felt. Instead, try to give an example that illustrates a difference of opinion or misunderstanding that you resolved through discussion.

"When I was working as a senior account executive for a large advertising firm, we had quite a difficult office manager. He was generally an asset to the company, but could at times be quite snappy when he was very busy. On one occasion, one of the junior members of my team came to me in tears. She had asked him for help to prepare a presentation for a client but he had been unhelpful and even shouted and called her some unpleasant names. At that point, I decided that we could no longer tolerate his behaviour – so I asked him to come out for lunch with me, so that we could talk away from the office. I gave him some tough feedback on how nasty he could get when he was under pressure. However, I emphasised that he was a very valuable member of our team and that we respected his ability to sort out office issues very quickly. So we didn't want to lose him. On hearing this feedback, he was initially quite defensive and refused to listen. But I gave him more specific examples of when he had been quite vicious to other people and gradually the penny dropped – he was genuinely horrified at his own behaviour under stress. Very quickly after that, we all saw a change in his behaviour. He became more conscious of his own behaviour, deliberately trying to be more considerate at all times."

Whatever your response, remember that (as with all competency-based questions), you must be ready to talk at length about exactly what you said or did. Other questions that the interviewer might use to probe further your style of dealing with difficult people include:

◆ "Why was this person difficult? What impact did this person have on your work?"
◆ "When you confronted this person, could you describe in more detail exactly what you said?"
◆ "What were your options in trying to change this person's mind?"

Can you give me an example of when you have influenced someone or changed their mind? What was the situation? And how did you change their mind?

Choose an example of a peer, rather than a subordinate, that you have influenced. Claiming to have changed the mind of someone who reported to you does not really count – as they really have little choice but to listen to you if you are their boss.

Or, if you have ever convinced a customer to buy from you or negotiated a better deal with a supplier – you could use that as your example of having influenced someone.

When constructing your response, remember that there are many different ways of changing a person's mind. Some people, for example, can be convinced by a logical argument backed by facts and figures. Others, however, may not respect what the facts say – they may need to be influenced by praise and compliments.

A candidate's response might be: "When I was a customer service manager for an overnight delivery company, we were invited to pitch for the contract to handle all of the deliveries for a very big business. We put together a good proposal but were told by the customer that we weren't the cheapest. We couldn't drop our price any further because it would have been unprofitable for us, so instead, I tried to persuade the customer that we would be a lower risk than our cheaper competitors. I invited him to see how our distribution centre worked. I gave him a tour of our centre and introduced him to the supervisors and staff. He saw our computerised tracking systems and watched packages being loaded onto vans. In the end, he liked what he saw and decided that our higher prices would ensure fewer breakages – so he signed a two-year contract with us that brought in over £110,000 over two years."

Give me an example of how you have gained buy-in from another person or persons

This question is no different to being asked to give an example of how you have persuaded someone that your ideas were right. Don't let yourself be put off by the concept of 'buy-in', which is simply organisational jargon for 'agreement'.

When have you managed to persuade someone more senior than you to change their mind?

This is just a variation of the basic question on how you have changed someone's mind. However, it is worth thinking about an occasion when you might have convinced someone more senior than yourself. Trying to influence upwards requires greater political sensitivity than influencing a peer – so try to reflect this in your response. For example, you may need to be subtler, by talking to a third person that has the ear of the senior person you are trying to win over.

Tell me about the most demanding customer/client situation you have faced and how you dealt with it

Customer service or client focus is often an important organisational competency. If you don't have external customers or clients, tell the interviewer that you don't have contact with them. However, everyone has internal customers – so think ahead of time about who your internal customers are.

Then this question simply becomes a version of the "tell me about a difficult person" question. Just make sure that your response includes a happy ending about how you resolved the situation to the satisfaction of both the customer but also your organisation.

CONSIDER HOW YOU JUDGE SITUATIONS, MAKE DECISIONS AND SOLVE PROBLEMS

Problems crop up in work every day of our working lives. To show that you are a good candidate, you need to be able to demonstrate to a prospective employer that you have good analytical and problem solving skills.

Tell me about a difficult problem and how you tackled it

Don't spend too much time describing the problem. Instead, talk about how you analysed the situation and how you tackled the problem. Your response should include:

♦ What the situation was.
♦ How you generated ideas for dealing with the problem.
♦ Which idea you ultimately chose.
♦ The outcome.

For instance: "The MD had issued instructions that each of the branch managers had to cut costs by 18%. As a branch manager at the time, everyone who worked for me knew that this probably meant making some of them redundant. However, I gathered the team together and ran a big brainstorming session, throwing dozens of ideas on to flip charts. One of the suggestions was that we could partition off part of the branch and sub-let the space to another company. I thought it was a good idea, so I set up a project team to explore how it would work. The team identified that it should work and we called in contractors to put up a dividing wall, refurbish the space and fill it with new office furniture and equipment. Then we advertised in the local press and managed to get a company to take the space. In the end, we managed to reduce our costs by 23%, which meant no redundancies at all."

Describe a situation when you had a difficult decision to make. What choices did you have and how did you eventually decide which one to take?

Many candidates say that the decision to leave a particular company to take up a new job is particularly difficult for them. However, if at all possible, it is better to talk about a decision that ultimately benefited your employer at the time.

This is a question with a couple of parts. In order to show an interviewer that you can make good decisions, an ideal answer would include at least some of the following steps:

◆ Gathering further information to understand the situation properly; you did not jump to conclusions too quickly.

◆ Involving other people to check that your information was correct or seeking their participation to get ideas on how to tackle the problem.

◆ Making a list of possible options for tackling the problem.

◆ Weighing up the pros and cons of each of the options.

◆ Determining the best of the options – probably with input from other colleagues, to ensure that you are not taking a risk that no one else agrees with.

Describe to me a situation when you made a bad decision

This question may be asked as a follow-up after you have given a good response to the preceding question on a difficult decision that you made. The interviewer is trying to probe a decision that did not go to plan.

A good answer might admit that the *outcome* of the decision was wrong – but that there was nothing wrong with the way in which you came to your decision. Perhaps you were under severe time pressure and were faced with either making a quick decision or losing a significant opportunity altogether. Or maybe you were forced to take a decision where there was no clear right or wrong. In either case, try to describe a situation where the outcome had a relatively minor effect on your company – as opposed to a disastrous impact.

For instance: "This was two years ago, when our company had been very busy setting up overseas offices in Europe. Anyway, we had been so busy all year that we had neglected to plan our Christmas party. It was coming up to the end of November and we hadn't decided on a venue. I volunteered to research a shortlist of restaurants or hotels that could accommodate 70 employees and their partners. So I phoned about 40 venues and it dawned on me that almost everywhere that we could afford was booked up. There were only two hotels that could take us at such short notice. Unfortunately, there simply wasn't time to consult everyone else in the company, so I went for a quick look around the two venues and chose one. It wasn't our best ever Christmas party – the food wasn't terribly good and the band played music that was suited for a much older crowd. But at least we had a party, so I stand by my decision because it was the best that I could find at such short notice."

Are you willing to take risks?

You might want to start by saying that: "It depends how you define risks. I would never endanger anyone else. But I am willing to take calculated business risks when I have weighed up the pros and cons of a situation. For example . . ."

And then continue along similar lines as the preceding question on making a bad decision. Again, the outcome of your decision may have been wrong – but given the incomplete information or limited time that you had, it was the best that you could do.

SUMMARY

◆ Go back to the job advert and job description to identify the skills or competencies that the interviewer is likely to ask you about.

◆ Think of specific examples of how you have motivated yourself and achieved benefits on behalf of your employer.

◆ Be ready to talk about particular instances when you have dealt with awkward people.

◆ Consider how you analysed situations, came to decisions and solved problems.

◆ Do not forget to think about the technical competencies for your job too.

◆ Prepare to give a lot of detail about every single example if the interviewer asks for it.

5

Talking about Your Personal Qualities

In this Chapter . . .

◆ Talking in general terms about yourself
◆ Being able to work with other people
◆ Being able to work on your own
◆ Dealing with hypothetical questions
◆ Being asked to define success

The competency-based questions that we covered in the previous chapter are very specific. But many questions ask you to talk in very general terms to the point of almost being vague. Many of these questions are very common, so do not skimp out now – keep reading on and thinking about how you would respond to each question.

MANY QUESTIONS ASK YOU FOR YOUR OWN OPINIONS ABOUT YOURSELF

Responding to questions that ask you to rate yourself or to evaluate yourself as others see you need to be handled with some subtlety. When talking about what you bring to an employer, there is a fine line between confidence and arrogance, so tread carefully. Similarly, when talking about your negative points and weaknesses, very little separates the sufficiently honest candidate from the foolishly honest candidate.

What is your greatest strength?

From your analysis of the job advert and job description, you will by now have figured out the key skills or competencies that are required for this particular role. So answering the question should be a breeze. Talk about one of these key skills, and, to hammer your point home, offer a brief example of how you have used the skill at work.

A candidate applying for a job as an investment analyst might begin by saying: "I think that my greatest strength is my ability to take in complex company financial information, build a spreadsheet to analyse its profitability, and make a decision very quickly as to whether the company would be a good venture or not. For example . . ."

And what is your greatest weakness?

If you get asked about your strengths, you *will* get asked about your weaknesses or development needs. However, candidates who are unable to come up with any weaknesses at all are often viewed with suspicion – are you claiming to be an angel of perfection? Instead, try to:

◆ Think about a couple of minor weaknesses that show that you are not perfect.
◆ Be ready to describe what actions or activity you are taking to improve or develop yourself.

For example: "I know that I can very quickly get frustrated when people don't make decisions. However, now that I am aware of it, I try to remember that colleagues may need time to think something through before giving me an answer."

But don't try to turn your weaknesses into strengths. Two examples that seem to re-occur are: "One of my weaknesses is that I'm a bit of a perfectionist – I tend to spend longer than necessary making sure that things are perfect." When I hear a candidate mention that, I just think that they've read it from a book. Another poor example of a weakness to cite is: "You might say I don't suffer fools gladly – I can't tolerate poor quality or lack of effort from other people." Again, it sounds too rehearsed.

What are your three biggest strengths and three biggest weaknesses?

Just a variation on the basic strengths and weaknesses question. It pays to plan ahead to have at least three or four strengths up your sleeve and a similar number of weaknesses, in case the interviewer insists on a certain number.

How would your colleagues/team/boss describe you?

Although you may be tempted to present a rounded picture of how your colleagues see you – you should try to get away with treating this question as if you had been asked, "What would your colleagues say are your strengths?" There is no benefit in mentioning weaknesses unless the interviewer specifically asks for them.

Simply talk about two or three of the key skills or competencies that are required of the job. If you can, though, try to back up your claims with any objective evidence that you may have on how colleagues have described you – such as from an appraisal, or from a 360-degree feedback report.

A gym instructor being interviewed for a job at a health club might say: "I think that my colleagues would say that I am very client-focused. I don't just stand around, waiting for members of the gym to come ask me questions. I wander around the gym, observing how they are getting on, chatting and offering advice. In fact, when the members of the gym were asked to rate the five instructors in the gym, I got a 4.5 rating out of 5."

How would you rate yourself as . . . ?

You could be asked to rate yourself as a team player, a researcher, a leader, or just about anything else. Obviously you need to start by saying that you are a very good team player, researcher, leader etc. – don't let modesty get in the way of making a good impression on the interviewer. The secret then is to back up your assertion with a short example that demonstrates that you are as good as you say.

"I'd say that I was one of the best technicians in our company. For example . . ."

Be careful, though, not to make extravagant claims unless you have evidence to support it – such as having won an award or having received the most sales commission out of your peer group.

What unique skills would you bring to our company?

A tricky question, as the interviewer is effectively asking you what you have that the other candidates do not have. If you know that you have some technical skills that very few candidates have, this is your opportunity to talk about them. However, if you are not sure that you have any skills that are unique to you and no one else, you could try a different approach – talk about the fact that you possess a combination of skills and determination that, taken together, are unique.

BEING ABLE TO WORK WITH OTHER PEOPLE IS A KEY SKILL

Teams are supposed to create something that is greater than the sum of their parts. But can you show the interviewer that you can navigate the minefield of disagreements, politicking and outright arguments that happen in most teams?

Would you say that you have good influencing skills?

Of course say: "yes". However, it is very easy to talk in abstract terms about how good you are at influencing and persuading others. Treat this like a competency-based question and continue by providing an example as proof of your skill.

How good are you at handling conflict?

Likewise, give an example as if you had been asked a competency-based question.

How do you take personal criticism?

You need to show the interviewer that you can take constructive criticism without taking offence or reacting defensively to it. "As long as the criticism is fair and constructive, I try to listen to it, thank them for their candid feedback, and modify my future behaviour accordingly."

The canny interviewer might follow up by asking: "Can you describe to me a situation in which you were criticised?" So make sure that you have an example up your sleeve too. However, avoid giving an example that involves lateness, absenteeism or aggressive behaviour – as these can signal to the interviewer that you are a troublesome employee. Better examples concern skills – such as presentation or computing skills – that you may have lacked at one point in your career, but which you have since worked on and have had some success in improving.

This job will require you to work with people from very different backgrounds to yourself – how will you cope?

Variations on this question could ask you how you work with people from 'very different educational backgrounds', 'different cultures' or 'different countries'. Whatever form the question takes, the best way to answer this is to provide an example to show that you have worked with people who are very different from yourself.

Everyone has worked with someone who is different – you just need to think hard enough for an example. Perhaps your boss was actually much younger than you. Perhaps your colleague spoke English as a second language. Or maybe you were working alongside a team of scientists, actuaries, or lecturers who were all much more highly qualified than you were. Whatever the situation, you could emphasise that you not only had a good working relationship, but also became good friends.

How do you respond to authority?

If an interviewer is asking you this question, it might be because the organisation is quite hierarchical – each employee knows their level and there might be rules on how you deal with people who are more senior than yourself.

An answer that shows your respect for authority might be: "I have no problem at all with authority. I like to know what my reporting line is and I realise that a big part of my job is satisfying the demands that my line manager will make upon me. If I were to be offered this job, I would really appreciate sitting down with my manager to establish how he or she likes to be communicated with, and how I should escalate problems should I encounter them."

What was the greatest failing of your last boss? And how did you compensate for it?

Speaking ill of your previous boss could reflect badly on you – so resist the temptation to talk at length about his or her faults. Try deflecting the question by emphasising the good qualities of your boss.

For example: "I can't say that there is much wrong with my boss – he has a lot of experience and has coached me in many ways, especially in my ability to present confidently in front of large groups of people."

However, if the interviewer pursues the matter and asks you to think of something, you could describe some relatively minor weakness of your boss that required very little effort on your part to compensate for.

"I wouldn't say that this is a major fault – it is more of a quibble. My current boss can be very forgetful. Often, you can tell him something and he can forget it even on the same day. So I have learned not to rely on him to remember times and dates of meetings. Instead, I always send him an email and send a copy to his secretary, so that she can politely manage his schedule."

Then perhaps reinforce the fact that you had a good relationship with your boss by finishing with another positive statement – "but this relatively minor weakness was far outweighed by the fact that he gave me a lot of responsibility" or "but I don't want to blow this weakness out of proportion, as he also taught me a lot about project management and writing press releases".

BEING ABLE TO WORK INDEPENDENTLY IS IMPORTANT TOO

Although employers appreciate the ability to work with other people, it goes without saying that you need to demonstrate that you are able to work on your own, without continual guidance and reassurance too.

Do you prefer to work on your own or with other people?

You do not want to give the impression that you are capable of only one but not the other. However, the 'right' answer depends on the nature of the job. Before the interview, you should have figured out whether you would be spending most of your time working on your own, or in a team with other people. Two examples are as follows:

♦ "I'm quite willing to work on my own when necessary – once I understand a task, I can soldier on until it is done. However, I prefer to work with a team – as I like to bounce ideas off other people and it makes the work more stimulating."

♦ "I'm happy to work with other people when I need to – I think I listen to what other people have to say and can make a contribution to group discussions too. However, I am applying for this job because I enjoy working by myself. I like having the freedom to think about a problem and come up with solutions on my own."

Would you say that you are reliable?

Of course you should say that you are reliable. However, you need to be able to give a response that makes you stand out from the other candidates. Employers worry about lateness, absenteeism from work and forgetfulness. As a consequence, punctuality, dependability and a willingness to work overtime to meet deadlines are valued traits.

Use an example to illustrate why you believe you are reliable. "There used to be five of us running the helpdesk. We were supposed to open at 9.00am for queries, but we also provided early cover from 7.30am. I'm proud to say that in the two-and-a-half years I worked there, I didn't miss any of my early shifts – I always either turned up on time or managed to swap my shift with someone else beforehand."

Can you work under pressure?

Before answering this question, you need to figure out how much pressure you think the job entails. For example, a journalist for a daily newspaper, a financial trader, or an air traffic controller might respond by saying: "I positively thrive on pressure. I couldn't do a job where I had to sit and watch the clock ticking by every day. I like to know that each day is going to be very different, with its own set of decisions to make and problems to solve."

However, if you are applying for a job where you would expect there to be more order in your day and less moment-to-moment pressure, you might want to talk a bit about how you plan and organise, in order to avoid last minute crunches. "I sit down and look at my workload at the start of each week in order to figure out which tasks I need to do on which days. I use a Gantt chart to keep up-to-date with projects that I am working on. However, when things do occasionally hit the fan, I resolve myself to the fact that it might be a late night in the office."

How do you cope with stress?

This differs from the previous question on whether you can handle pressure, because it is asking you how you deal with the tension that can result from tight deadlines.

Even though your preferred method of relaxing may be to have a glass of wine when you get home, this could be frowned upon by an uptight interviewer. What is socially acceptable in one organisation may be deemed inappropriate by another firm – so this is where your research into the culture and prevailing attitudes in the company will help you. A firm of closely-knit management consultants, for example, might regard having a drink in the evening with colleagues as not only acceptable but almost a requirement of working there. They might snigger behind closed doors at candidates who profess to meditating or enjoying quiet reading. I agree that these sorts of attitudes are hardly fair – but I'm afraid that not all interviewers are fair.

Physical exercise or competitive sports are very socially acceptable methods of releasing stress. For example: "I play squash two or three times a week, which really helps me to unwind and get ready for another day at work."

Do you pay attention to detail?
Again, this is a ridiculous question as you are hardly going to say "no". A good response would include an example of when you have paid attention – perhaps while proofreading a document – and spotted a mistake that would otherwise have cost the company time or money.

How much experience do you have of managing budgets?
In an age when employers are looking to keep costs low, this is an opportunity for you to shine if you have had such experience. In your response, talk about the biggest budget that you have managed and be specific about how you handled it.

"I was the budget holder for our department. We had a cost budget of £95,000 per annum. I allowed my team to spend at their discretion up to a £150 limit. But for anything over that, they had to come to see me. If they wanted approval for anything over £1,000, I insisted that they write a business case to justify the spend."

How are you with new technology?

If you are applying for a technical job, then be prepared to talk about the technical wizardry that you can extract from your systems – macros that you have written, speed dials that you have devised, or shortcuts that you regularly employ. However, most employers are more interested in basic computer literacy. In particular, employers worry that older candidates (born earlier than 1965 or so) may struggle with even the basics of using a computer, or other systems such as voicemail – especially in an era when the majority of senior managers would at least draft their own documents on a computer, for a secretary to tidy up.

If you have particular experience of any software pro-grammes such as Lotus Notes, AmiPro, Microsoft Word, and so on that you have used, then talk about the sorts of tasks that you can do with them. For example: "I have created a database of our clients' details which has allowed me to create a mailshot and send them tailored fliers on a quarterly basis."

But because you can never be sure what systems your inter-viewer's organisation may use, you should also emphasise that you are a quick learner on new packages: "I also learn quickly. For example, I had never built a spreadsheet until I joined my last company – and now I can build simple financial models to keep track of our monthly sales against budget."

How is your absenteeism/attendance record?

You will have to be honest here, as this is something that many employers check when they ask for references. If you have had a problem, then give a good reason to explain why it occurred at the time – and why it will not happen again.

For instance: "I did suffer from a fairly serious virus about 18 months ago, but it cleared up over a year ago and I have not had any problems since – and it's something that my references will also confirm."

Ours is a long-hours culture. Is that a problem for you?

This may be a trick question – what they call long hours might not be what you consider to be long (or vice versa). Encourage the interviewer to quantify what he or she means by asking, "what exactly do you call long hours?"

You could tailor your response accordingly. "I understand that this is a demanding job that I am applying for. But I really do thrive on the challenge of this sort of work – so I am willing to work whatever hours it takes to get the work done."

If you have worked similarly long hours in the past, you should definitely cite this experience as well.

DON'T GET CAUGHT OUT BY HYPOTHETICAL QUESTIONS

Untrained interviewers may ask you hypothetical questions that usually include the word 'if . . .' or the phrase 'how would you . . . ?' in the sentence somewhere. Again, they are trying to get inside your head and figure out what makes you tick.

There are hundreds of possibilities for hypothetical questions, but here are some of the most common ones. Most of the hypothetical questions you may get asked will be variations on these.

How would you respond to change?

'Change management' is a big buzzword in the workplace at the moment, as organisations continually revamp how they operate in order to compete more effectively. So employers want to hear that you are adaptable and flexible to change.

It is even better if you can give an example of how you have been involved in making change happen in the past. "We had a team of management consultants review our computer systems. I volunteered to join the internal consulting team to manage the relationship with the consultants and worked with them for six months."

What action would you take if you disagreed with the decision of your manager?

Saying that you would immediately speak up could mark you out as a troublemaker. So couch your response carefully.

"I would speak up. But there are times when tact is required – for example, if my manager were to say something in a meeting that I felt was wrong, I would wait until we had a moment alone to try to put him right. At the end of the day though, I recognise that a manager is entitled to make decisions that I may not always agree with. As long as I feel that I have been given a fair chance to air my views, I would have to go along with their decision."

Naturally, an interviewer may ask you for a specific example of when this might have happened too.

If you spotted a colleague doing something unethical or illegal, what would you do?

The interviewer is not asking you what you would do if your colleague were doing something that you merely disagreed with – ethics and legality are in a bigger league than mere differences of opinion. You must state that you would act immediately to put a stop to any unethical or illegal activity.

"I would try to document the details of the incident and try to collect any physical evidence. Then I would report it immediately to my line manager or HR."

What would you do if a colleague came to you in tears?

Your answer should recognise that support for your colleagues can come in various forms. Listening skills and empathy are as important as being able to offer practical assistance.

"Naturally, I would take them aside and figure out what it was that was upsetting them so. If it were something that I could help with – for example getting them over a difficult deadline – I would try to offer them my time. But if it was a personal problem, I would try to listen and offer my sympathies and a shoulder to lean on."

What would you do if your partner phoned you to tell you that your son or daughter had taken ill in the middle of the day?

A silly question – because it depends on the illness (and assumes that you have a partner and child).

"I would ring home to find out what the situation was. In my experience, many children's ailments only require soothing words and bed rest that my partner could take care of. But if it was something serious that required immediate hospitalisation, then I would hope that my employer would understand the need for me to take half a day off work."

If I told you that you're not suitable for this job, what would you do?

In reality, you may feel like throttling the interviewer with an item of his or her own clothing after all of the effort you have put into preparing for the interview. However, a tactic that is more likely to get you the job may be to say: "I would respond by asking you why you think I'm not suitable for the job. Are you saying that I am not suitable for this job?"

Hopefully then, the interviewer should tell you about their concerns, allowing you to respond to each of these in turn.

SOME INTERVIEWERS LIKE TO ASK YOU FOR DEFINITIONS OF KEY CONCEPTS

Some interviewers try to figure out whether you have certain skills by asking you to define certain concepts. Typically, it is the not-very-good interviewers who will ask you such questions – because anyone could just learn these definitions from a textbook. But let's keep that just between you and me. After all, if you want the job, you may just have to play the interviewer's game.

Define leadership

Your answer must vary according to the sort of organisation that you are applying to. Do think about the culture and leadership style of the organisation that is interviewing you before answering. In very simple terms, we could think of organisations as either being tortoises or hares.

◆ Tortoises – organisations that are more bureaucratic and traditional in their approaches, such as the civil service, organisations in the public sector, and many utilities and airlines. They tend to think of managers as people who should respect the hierarchy and teach the employees below them to abide by systems, processes and rules. Risk-taking may even be frowned on in such companies.

◆ Hares – more progressive organisations that value empowerment instead of control. Companies that are mainly driven by profit will see themselves in this category.

A response for a candidate applying to a tortoise might start along the lines of: "Leadership is a process of managing the team to get the job done. It involves delegating clear instructions to the team, and checking with them to make sure that they understand their tasks and are making progress."

A response for a hare organisation might be: "I see leadership as a process of creating and communicating a vision, then supporting and motivating my team to achieve that vision. Good leadership requires being able to develop individuals and build the team so that they can tackle increasingly greater problems and opportunities."

How would you define teamwork?

There are many aspects of teamwork. However, a good response might draw upon some of the following elements:

◆ Common goals that are understood by all members of the team.

◆ Involvement of all team members. Everyone on the team, no matter how junior or inexperienced, must have a role.

◆ Honesty and open communication. An opportunity for everyone to air his or her views and be listened to.

◆ A feeling of commitment from members of the team that what they are doing is important.

How would you define success?

In devising your answer, make sure that you do not mention only personal success. Your answer should also include reference to the success of your team or organisation.

For example: "Success for me is about knowing that I have made a difference both to myself and my organisation. I like to make a difference to myself by developing my own skills. And I like to make a difference to my organisation by achieving good results."

If you want to allude to financial reward, you could add a statement such as: "If I achieve these two things, then I think it is only fair that I should also be rewarded well for it."

What's your definition of a good employer?

Strictly speaking, this question is not asking about your personal qualities, but it makes sense to mention it here. What the interviewer is trying to figure out is whether your definition matches how the interviewer would describe their company.

SUMMARY

◆ Think about the organisation's competencies before describing your strengths.

◆ Prepare to talk about a few relatively minor weaknesses.

◆ Emphasise your team qualities as well as your ability to get a job done by yourself.

◆ Try to answer hypothetical questions by giving a concrete example whenever possible.

◆ Think about the specific organisation that is interviewing you before answering questions about intangibles such as leadership and teamwork.

6

Fending Off Trick Questions

In this Chapter . . .

◆ Stupid questions that interviewers sometimes ask
◆ Responding positively to negative questions
◆ How to open up closed questions
◆ Handling attempts to throw you off balance
◆ Smiling through illegal questions

Skilled interviewers know that they should put candidates at their ease and get them to talk about how they have used their skills and experience in the past. Unfortunately, many managers are asked to interview without having ever been trained.

It is these unskilled interviewers who could ask you all sorts of weird questions. And this chapter shows you some of the more common ones that they ask because, quite frankly, they do not know any better.

SOME QUESTIONS JUST SHOULDN'T BE ASKED IN INTERVIEWS

Some questions can't possibly tell the interviewer anything about your ability to do the job – but obviously the interviewer thinks that it is a good question. So you have no choice really but to have a shot at responding briefly to the question, then trying to turn the question to your advantage to show off some skill.

Do you read much? What was the last book you read?

Don't be caught lying – if you are going to say that you have read a key business book, then be ready to answer technical questions about the content of the book. However, few interviewers will expect you to have read a business book. Just be ready to discuss the plot or contents of a book that you have read. Ideally, the book should have improved you in at least some small way.

For example: "The book talks about the plight of the servant classes in turn-of-the-century China. It's a very humbling description of the effects of poverty and injustice."

What was the last film you saw?

It does not matter what the last film you saw was. Just be prepared to talk briefly about the plot and why you saw it.

After naming the film, for instance: ". . . which was a big budget action adventure movie. I watch all sorts of things from independent French films to romantic comedies, but on this occasion I wanted something escapist to watch."

See this pencil I'm holding? Sell it to me

This is a common question – and rarely asked of salespeople. You could be asked to sell just about anything that the interviewer has within reach – from a lamp to the chairs you are both sitting on. The interviewer is trying to put you on the spot, testing how you respond to the sorts of unexpected pressures that can crop up at work as well as your ability to communicate and sell ideas.

Think of the interviewer as a potential customer for the object that you are being asked to sell, and follow the following three steps:

1. Ask the interviewer about his or her needs and exposure to objects of this sort. For example, if you were selling a chair: "How would you rate the chairs around your house or in the office? Do you need to sit at a desk for many hours of the day?"
2. Talk about key *features* of the object. For example, a chair may be comfortable. A pen may be filled with red ink.
3. Discuss some of the key *benefits* of the object. A comfortable chair could help the interviewer to work for longer without getting backache. A red ink pen could help him to correct documents more easily without confusing the corrections with the original text.

If you were an animal, what would you be?

The interviewer has probably read a 'pop psychology' book claiming that candidates can be rated based on the types of animals they would describe themselves as. This is a ridiculous question as there is no link between job performance and types of animals.

Unfortunately, you need to play along with this amateur Freud. Select a suitably noble animal such as a lion, eagle, wolf, etc. and go on to relate how its characteristics relate to your ability to do the job. For example, you could argue that an elephant can 'cope with a heavy workload' or that a Labrador 'picks up skills quickly'. Resist the temptation to choose an animal with comical or sinister qualities such as a kangaroo or a snake.

There are endless variations on this question. I have also heard an interviewer ask: "If you were a type of vehicle, what would you be?" Again, think about certain cars that are known for their reliability or speed etc.

Tell me a story

Ideally, you should tell a story about your career, including examples of the skills that the interviewer is looking for. Perhaps first ask, "Can I tell you the story of my career?"

However, if the interviewer insists that you tell a story about something outside work, try to tell a story about something that you have achieved – whether it is learning a musical instrument, to designing an extension for your house.

If you could meet anyone living or dead, who would it be?

Pick someone who has characteristics or skills that would be desirable in the job you are applying for – such as a notable business leader. However, resist citing the really well known business gurus such as Tom Peters or Warren Bennis – as that could make you sound clichéd. Politicians can also be risky choices if you do not know the political leanings of your interviewer. Also steer clear of poets, humanitarians or artists – unless you can argue that they have traits that you would use for this particular job.

For example: "I would like to meet Arnaud Gasnier, who was the chief executive of Matazar, the European retailer. The firm grew from five shops to 80 shops and saw sales grow by over 1000% in six years. I'd love to pick his brains about his vision for the retail industry."

Who do you admire, and why?

I have said it before, but I shall say it again: think about the skills or competencies that the interviewing organisation is looking for. Perhaps you could talk about a tutor or previous boss who was a good role model for one of those skills. Giving an example of a manager that you have worked for will also give the interviewer the impression that you are respectful of those who are senior to you.

For example: "My previous manager was a really good role model. She was on the fast track to partnership at the firm, but almost invariably managed to squeeze her workload into a 9am to 6pm day. She was very focused on her work during the day, which allowed her to have a good work–life balance too."

What kind of manager would you like to work for?

Your answer depends on what you know about the organisation. For example, if you think that the organisation is driven by strict rules and procedures, you might say: "I would like to have a manager who will give me clear instructions and expect me to be able to deliver good results."

Perhaps the organisation is known for its creativity and giving employees a great deal of autonomy: "I'd like to work for a manager who will listen to my ideas and give me the authority and responsibility to do a good job." Or maybe the interviewer will be your prospective manager. So a good answer would change according to what you think the inter-viewer wants to hear.

SOME QUESTIONS ARE PHRASED NEGATIVELY TO BEGIN WITH

Some questions start by making a negative statement about you, and invite you to fight your way uphill to impress the interviewer. Because these questions can be convoluted, you should take a few seconds to ensure that you have under-stood the question properly before responding.

I don't understand why you think you are the right person for this job

You might want to ask the interviewer why he or she thinks so: "Can I ask why you think that?" or "Could you be a bit more specific please? What exactly are your doubts?"

If the interviewer says no, you could begin your reply by saying: "I have to say that I'm disappointed that you think that. I think that I am the right person because of the following reasons . . ." And then cite a few skills or charac-teristics that you know the interviewer is looking for.

However, if the interviewer does give you any reasons why he or she doubts you are right for the job, you should take each of those points in turn and give an example to alleviate their anxieties.

Why do you think that you are better than the other candidates?

The question asserts that you think you are better than the other candidates – and you need to correct that assertion. "I haven't met the other candidates, so I can only talk about myself. What I hope I have done is to impress you with my track record of results. In particular, I think I have three main strengths . . ." And so on.

Do you like regular hours and routine working patterns?

It depends on what you know of the organisation. Is it the sort of organisation where the work may be very repetitive – in which case you should reply with something like: "Yes, I like to get comfortable with a job so that I can do it well."

However, if the job requires travel, changing deadlines and pace, you might say: "No, I like to have new challenges and variety that will keep me from getting bored but also improve my skill set. That's why I am interested in this job."

Do you mind paperwork and other bureaucratic practices?

The interviewer might be trying to hint that the job will involve a lot of administrative work.

A good reply might be to say: "I don't mind it. I realise that doing things properly and having a good paper trail are important parts of the job."

Do you mind travelling much?

Simply answering "no" is not enough. Perhaps you could say, "It is part of the job and I am used to it. I find that I can catch up with my reading on trains."

If you do mind, keep your mouth shut until you have been offered the job and have the opportunity to negotiate exactly how often you will have to travel.

Have you ever broken rules to get a job done?

Be careful here, as there is a critical difference between breaking a rule once to achieve a benefit to the organisation and breaking rules on multiple occasions because you find rules restrictive.

When answering, explain that you broke a rule only because there was an opportunity or challenge to which you had to react quickly – the organisation would have lost out if you had not broken the rules. However, finish by saying that you then went to your boss or whoever you needed to, to tell them about the incident.

For instance: "I have broken the rules – but only because the rules were stopping me from achieving what I knew my boss wanted. I had been asked to get quotes from three companies on the costs of printing a brochure that we needed for the end of the week. I am supposed to get her to sign off on expenditure over £1000, but she had been called into a meeting. The cheapest quote came in at about £1200 –

but I gave them the go-ahead anyway, because otherwise we would not have had the brochures done by the end of the week."

All of us have personality defects. What is yours?

A personality defect is a very strong term. Perhaps you could begin your answer by saying: "I wouldn't say that I have anything as strong as a personality defect. However, I do have areas that I know I could improve on. For example . . ."

And then continue as if you had been asked to list your weaknesses.

Do you take work home with you in the evenings or at weekends?

A question that tries to trap you into admitting that you are ineffective during the day and need to catch up in the evenings and at weekends.

A candidate might respond by saying: "I very rarely find the need to. I prefer to get it all done in the office because you have everything that you need to hand and you can bounce ideas off colleagues."

Why did you not achieve more in your last job?

The interviewer may be trying to provoke you into reacting emotionally. However, a calm candidate might say: "I don't see achievement as solely measured by promotion up the hierarchy. It has been more important to me to be given challenging work and to be learning new skills. However, I am now ready to move on because I do feel that I could be given more responsibility as well as new challenges."

DON'T JUST ANSWER "YES" OR "NO" TO CLOSED QUESTIONS

Technically, you could get away with answering only "yes" or "no" to closed questions. However, you will give the interviewer a much clearer picture of your skills and fit with the organisation if you continue by giving an example to support and explain your "yes" or "no".

Do you ever have any doubts about your own ability to do the job?

Insecurity is a deeply unattractive trait in potential employees. Who wants to work with someone who needs constant reassurance? However, be careful not to sound arrogant in your response.

Do you regard it as a weakness to lose your temper?

A "yes" could imply that no one should ever lose his or her temper. But a "no" could imply that you lose your temper regularly.

So explain briefly. For example: "I can't think of an occasion when I have personally lost my temper at work. However, I recognise that we're all only human – it could happen to me in the future. So I try to be patient and understanding of the reasons why someone else may be angry."

Good morning. Would you like a cup of coffee before we start?

Not a trick question. If you would like to, then do accept a drink, as you may be talking for a few hours and need to moisten your mouth and throat.

A FEW INTERVIEWERS LIKE TO INTERROGATE CANDIDATES

In the bad old days of interviewing, quite a few interviewers used to think that giving candidates a hard time and deliberately putting them under stress was a good idea. Luckily, most interviewers know better – although there may still be one or two interviewers who haven't heard that stress interviews are out.

If you are faced with an aggressive interviewer, you must keep your composure. Responding to anger with anger will only escalate the situation. Remember that you want to be offered a job, so you need to hide your irritation. Be calm, take your time, and focus on answering the question.

Quite frankly, I don't think you have enough experience of . . .

If the interviewer expresses a concern about a skill or experience that you do actually have (but he or she just does not know about), you should give an example to make it clear to the interviewer that you do possess it.

However, if you do not have the required skill or experience, you would need to emphasise your willingness and ability to learn. Give an example of a related skill that you picked up very quickly.

For example: "It's true that I haven't much experience of running workshops. But when I joined my previous company, I had never given a performance appraisal either. But I asked personnel to send me on a course and I did some reading and talking to other team leaders about it. By the end of the year, I got an award for being one of the top 10% of team leaders in the company. So I do learn quickly."

Have you ever been fired?

The best answer would be to say "no". However, if you cannot, then you will need to have good reasons why it happened.

There are two good ways of getting around this question:

1. By blaming your underperformance on personal circumstances such as ill health or relationship difficulties. However, stress that those circumstances are now completely in the past.
2. By admitting to having made the wrong career decision in joining that company. For example, you thought that the job would involve X and Y. However, the job actually involved a lot of A, B and C. So you lost your motivation and deserved to be fired. In order to get your next job, you will need to do your research so that you can convince the interviewer that you understand the demands of this job and therefore could in no way lose your enthusiasm for the job.

What keeps you up at night?

In reality, most people have a combination of both personal and professional worries. However, you may want to downplay the extent to which you agonise over work-related issues:

"I don't think anything keeps me up at night, to be honest. I have concerns, obviously – but for the most part I feel that

I am in control of my life. At work, I want to do a good job and feel that people respect me for my work. But I wouldn't say that these trouble me overly."

Aren't you overqualified (or have too much experience) for this job?

The employer may be worried that you might get bored with the job and move on quickly. If you agree that you are overqualified, you could try explaining that you are looking for a better work/life balance. There may have been too much travel or the hours were too long in your previous or current job – perhaps you have family or other personal commitments that mean you want to have some stability in your working life for a few years. You could try arguing that you want to join a smaller company where you can feel that you have a greater impact on what goes on.

How would you rate me as an interviewer?

It would be dangerous to express your honest opinion if the interviewer is boring you or asking the wrong sorts of questions! Be diplomatic and constructive if you want to make any small criticisms.

"You have been giving me a chance to talk about my skills and experience, so I'd say that you were doing a very good job. However, I hope you will give me some time today to ask you about the role and why you like this company."

SOME QUESTIONS ARE DOWNRIGHT ILLEGAL

Legal guidelines specifically prohibit certain questions that have no relevance to a candidate's ability to do the job. However, interviewers rarely ask illegal questions deliberately. They are more likely to be acting out of ignorance. But your choice of answer depends on how much you want the job. You may legally be entitled to refuse to answer the question, but you will embarrass the interviewer and reduce your chances of getting the job. Would you really want to try to prove discrimination in a court of law?

If you really want the job, you may just want to swallow your pride and answer the question.

Are you married?
Of course you want to say: "None of your bloody business!" But remember that the interviewer probably doesn't realise that he or she is asking an illegal question.

Whether you say "yes" or "no", finish by saying: "But I don't think that my marital status will affect my ability to do the job."

Then go on to give an example of why you would be able to succeed in the job.

What happens when you decide to have children?
Interviewers sometimes assume (incorrectly) that all women want to have children and that children would have an adverse effect on your motivation or ability to work.

You could answer: "Actually, I have no plans for having children – I don't see myself needing children to be ful-filled."

Or, given that few employees these days stay in jobs for longer than four or five years anyway: "I don't plan on having children for at least five more years, because I have certain career goals that I would like to achieve before I hit 35."

Or perhaps: "I have no current plans to have children. However, should I decide to have children, I will continue to work. A lot of my female colleagues in previous companies have taken the minimum period of maternity leave and have then returned to full-time work. And I would wish to do the same – as I think I would miss the buzz of work and having new business challenges on a daily basis."

Are you pregnant at the moment?

While you do not legally have to disclose the answer to this question, you may want to answer truthfully anyway. An employer could make your life very difficult for you if you lied when you knew that you were expecting.

Does your husband/wife/family mind you being away from home?

The fact that you are married should not affect your willingness to travel. However, rather than get into a debate about this fact, a married candidate might respond by saying: "I have always travelled extensively as part of my work – in fact I enjoy it – so my marital status really shouldn't be a cause of concern for you."

An unmarried candidate might make the best impression by just saying: "I'm not married, so this isn't a problem."

This job requires you to work on a Saturday/Sunday/particular day of the week. Does that cause any conflict with your religion?

Hopefully you will already have ascertained from your research before the interview that you might have to work on certain days. So if you decided to press ahead with the interview, you should be able to simply say, "not at all".

Does your religion mean you will need to take more holidays than other employees?

"No." If you must take certain religious holidays, explain that you will take these as part of your annual leave entitlement.

SUMMARY

◆ Remember that there are many untrained, unskilled interviewers who can ask questions that bear little relation to the job.

◆ Put up with these silly questions by smiling and trying to turn them to your advantage.

◆ Aim to mention a skill, competency or characteristic in every answer you give.

◆ Control your emotions or any anger you may feel when you are asked an illegal question. In 99% of cases, the interviewer is asking the question out of ignorance.

7

Handling Questions for Different Career Stages

In this Chapter . . .

◆ What questions do graduates get asked?
◆ Questions for non-graduates too
◆ How can managers prepare for interviews?
◆ Questions for candidates returning to work
◆ Fending off discrimination against older candidates

Interviewers do not like taking risks. Given a safe but boring candidate and a risky but potentially exciting candidate, many interviewers would take the boring candidate – the candidate who has been to a good university, has never been out of work, and who has a few good (but not too many) years of work experience behind them.

If you do not fit that safe but boring, middle-of-the-road profile, you will need to reduce the interviewer's anxiety levels and make him or her believe that you are not a risk at all. Interviewers have different questions for candidates at different stages of their career. Graduates and school leavers may have very little work experience that they can talk about. But you would expect a senior manager to be able to talk at length about major projects.

Which of the questions in this chapter are relevant to you?

QUESTIONS FOR GRADUATES OFTEN FOCUS ON MOTIVATION AND DRIVE

Interviewers sometimes report that they find it difficult to distinguish between graduates (or school leavers). In many cases, you will not have any relevant work experience. So they have to rely on your academic achievements and the decisions you have made so far, to judge whether you would be a good employee or not.

Why did you choose the university you went to?

The interviewer is trying to understand how you make decisions. Ideally, you would say that you chose your university in a systematic fashion – after considering a range of course options and the reputations of different universities, and visiting campuses to get a feel for the quality of accommodation, as well as social life.

Why did you choose the degree subject that you chose?

Again, like the previous question on your choice of university, the interviewer is interested in your ability to gather data and make informed decisions. A good response might mention that you did some research as to the practical nature of the course and by talking to lecturers and current students as to the content and relevance of the course to the world outside academia.

What have you learned at university?

Unless you did a vocational course, your degree subject will probably be of little interest to the interviewer. Instead, think about the skills that are required for the job. Then give three or four examples of relevant skills that you have picked up from university such as:

◆ Organising events and your fellow students.
◆ Raising funds for a society or charity, and managing a budget.
◆ Working in teams.
◆ Presenting information at seminars or lectures.
◆ Analysing data and writing reports.
◆ Etc.

What sorts of summer jobs have you had?

If your previous jobs have no relevance to the role that you are applying for, you could explain that you took those jobs because they were the best paying jobs that you could find that fitted your course schedule. Finish by sneaking in a skill or quality that your job taught you.

For instance: "I worked as a sales assistant at Curby's, a firm of electrical retailers. It was a very customer focused role – I had to listen to their needs and explain the features and benefits of products to persuade them to make a purchase."

INTERVIEWERS SOMETIMES GET FIXATED ON GRADUATES

Many job adverts ask for 'graduates' or 'graduate-calibre' candidates. If you have been invited to interview, then someone thinks you could do the job. Unfortunately, the person sifting CVs and application forms may not be the same person as the interviewer.

I think that this role requires a graduate

Even though you may have the skills and experience for the job, opinions such as this can be quite entrenched. So be tactful in trying to change the interviewer's mind. You could try (politely) asking the interviewer: "I hope you don't mind my asking, but exactly what skills or attributes are you looking for in a graduate applicant?"

When the interviewer responds, you can then compose an answer that shows you have each of those skills or attributes.

For example, a candidate might argue: "I can understand that university does develop people's ability to learn new concepts and evaluate them critically. However, I have practical experience, which has allowed me to hone these skills. For example . . ."

Why did you not go to university?

An employer may want to know what motivated you in the early part of your career. You must endeavour to show the interviewer that, even though you did not go to university, it was not because you do not see the value of learning.

In answering, you could potentially talk about:

◆ How personal circumstances meant that you needed to earn a living rather than run up debts studying.
◆ The fact that you wanted to join the workforce and feel

that you were developing practical skills, rather than the more abstract and esoteric skills that you might have picked up at university.

♦ That, at the tender age of 16 or 18, you did not have any interest in, or understand the importance of, further education. However, in later years, you realised its importance. Then go on to talk about personal improvement that you have undertaken since then – such as diplomas or other courses.

QUESTIONS FOR MANAGERS CONCENTRATE ON LEADERSHIP SKILLS

Managers have to interact with their teams in a very different way to how employees work together.

Are you a good manager?

Does the interviewer expect you to say "no"? Rather than just answering "yes", treat this as if it were a competency-based question. Provide an example to explain why you are a good manager. Perhaps you could talk about a situation such as:

♦ Coaching or developing the employees in your team.

♦ Splitting up an initially overwhelming task into different roles and responsibilities for the members of your team, and then helping them to complete the task.

♦ Being brought in to turn around an underperforming team.

♦ Creating a vision or business strategy for your department.

♦ Inspiring or motivating a team to achieve results.

Your reply should incorporate a brief explanation of the background to the example, as well as a description of what you did and the results achieved.

As an example: "I was brought into the organisation to turn the legal department from being a group of administrators into advisors to the other business units. The majority of my team had been there for over a decade and were reactive, as opposed to proactively offering help to our internal customers. I spent my first weeks getting to know the individuals in my team and understanding their strengths, weaknesses and aspirations. Then I set up weekly meetings with each of them to discuss how they could be more pro-active in providing advice to our internal customers. The team were very receptive, with the result that the business units now make decisions that are far less likely to cause legal complications."

Describe a tough time that you had in dealing with a member of your team

Don't fall into the trap of saying that you never had any problems in your entire career – no interviewer will believe you. The interviewer is looking for you to talk openly about how you tackled a difficult situation with an employee.

The worst thing that you could say here is that you used your seniority to force a member of your team to do it your way. Interviewers will more likely want to hear about how you:

◆ Coached and developed the individual – perhaps in formal meetings as well as informal mentoring, encouragement, and training courses that you sent the person on. Perhaps you also tried to restructure the department or changed the nature of the work to suit them better.

◆ Or decided to move the person, either to a job in another department that played to their strengths, or outside the company entirely. However, do emphasise that – once you had taken the decision to remove the individual – you balanced the need to be caring and empathetic with the need to ensure that there was no negative effect on the business.

What involvement have you had in writing business strategy?

Being able to 'think strategically' is an important skill in more senior roles. If you have had such experience, think about your involvement, the resulting strategy, and the impact of the strategy on the company.

How is your performance measured?

Be as specific as possible in your answer. Talking about specifics makes you more believable. Managers who are unable to talk about performance measurement may appear sloppy. Talk about the kinds of measures (e.g. revenue, profit margins, employee headcount, market share, customer or employee satisfaction indexes, quality etc.), but then be prepared to answer the question: "And how are you performing against those measures?"

For example: "I am currently measured on my ability to improve the gross margin for the products that I look after. The margin was 9% when I arrived, and I was targeted with improving it to 12.5% by January of the next year. However, I actually exceeded my target by improving the margin to 13.2% – which was primarily through revenue growth as opposed to cost cutting."

Can you tell me about your external network?

Managers are often expected to keep abreast of what is going on in terms of customer and competitor trends in the market. So be ready to talk not only about the market but also how you gather information on the market. What conferences or forums do you attend? To what extent do you keep in touch with ex-customers, ex-colleagues and managers in similar roles in other organisations?

Be ready to give an example of how you have used your network. The interviewer might ask you to: "Tell me about an example of a time when you have used your network to gain insight into a business problem."

How do you think you have added value to your company?

This is just another way of asking you about your greatest achievements. Think about benefits such as increases in market share, profits and revenues, quality or people satisfaction, or decreases in time or cost.

AFTER TIME AWAY FROM WORK, YOU MUST WORK HARD TO IMPRESS EMPLOYERS

Perhaps you were made redundant or took maternity leave for only a few months. Perhaps you took several years off to bring up a family or to recuperate from a serious illness.

Whatever your reasons, employers can be unfairly suspicious of time away from work.

Why did you leave your last job?

This question used to be a worry for candidates who had been made redundant. Today's job climate is very different from that of only ten years ago – there is no such thing as a "job for life" anymore, and redundancy is losing the stigma that was once attached to it. Honesty may therefore be the best policy.

For example: "The company needed to reduce its headcount by 15%. There were nearly 200 job losses in the UK alone, and that's why I find myself looking for a new job."

Why did they select you for redundancy?

When making staff redundant, many companies have a simple policy of 'last in, first out'. So, if you can, say that you were simply selected because you (and the others who were also made redundant) had a shorter tenure than the remaining members of the team.

Or you could argue that your role was made redundant due to a restructuring in the organisation, then explain that you did not want to take any of the roles that were made available to you, as they offered insufficient challenge.

Why have you been out of work for so long?

Finding a job takes time. Redundancy is often a good opportunity for many candidates to evaluate their goals in life and think about what they really want to be doing for the rest of their careers. Your response could reflect the fact that you have been doing a lot of thinking and research to identify the perfect role for you.

For example: "I realise now that I had been stagnating with Company X. When I was made redundant, I wanted to take a step back and think about the sort of role I wanted as well as the kind of company I wanted to work for. I was doing a lot of networking and talking to head hunters, to figure out what might be right for me."

I'm worried that your time away from the workforce may put you at a disadvantage

The interviewer may be worried that the reasons that took you out of work (e.g. young children, illness or failure to find a job) may crop up again in the future. Begin by asking: "If you don't mind me asking, what is it exactly that worries you?"

For example, if you have young children, you may have to deal with problems about their health or struggle to find good childcare and therefore be unreliable in turning up for work. If you had problems with your health in the past, perhaps the problem could return.

Once you understand the interviewer's concerns, you can counter them.

You've been working for yourself for some time now. Why do you want to be employed by a company again?

Not strictly a question that fits into the category of 'returning to work'. But still a question that interviewers ask of people who have spent any time working for themselves, perhaps as freelancers. Many interviewers think that setting up in business on one's own is a way to make more money – so anyone who decides to re-join a company must have failed to succeed at it.

Two ways out of this quandary are to mention:

◆ That you miss having colleagues to share ideas and the work with.
◆ The fact that you enjoy a particular core activity, but not the peripheral activities of running a business. For example: "I most enjoy designing. But when you are a freelancer, you spend so much of your time networking and trying to find new clients, and then having to send them invoices and chase payments. I now realise that I would rather focus on the design itself and let other people take care of business development and the administration."

DON'T LET INTERVIEWERS DISCRIMINATE UNFAIRLY AGAINST YOU IF YOU ARE OLDER

Even if your age is not on your CV, interviewers can estimate your age from dates that you took exams or attended university, or the length of time you have been in employment. For candidates who are 50+, interviewers may be concerned (usually unfairly) that you do not have the drive and motivation of a younger candidate.

However, remember to express your disagreement tactfully with the interviewer. Making a stand may make you feel better from a moral standpoint, but won't help your chances of getting the job.

This is a challenging role – are you sure you want to do it at this stage of your career?

We all want to make a mark in life, so respond by saying that you feel that there is still this one (or perhaps more) challenge(s) that you need to complete, so that you can feel that you have achieved something.

For instance: "I am now the Finance Director of one of the largest business units in the group. However, I still feel that I haven't achieved everything in my career that I set out to do. I have always wanted to be the Group FD of a FTSE 100 company because I would like to be able to say that I had a hand in a major cross-border acquisition."

When do you plan to retire?

Interviewers like to feel that they are going to get good value out of the people that they hire. So the best answer, if you are able to give it, would be: "Not for at least five years."

SUMMARY

◆ Understand that interviewers worry that candidates who do not have a standard career history may be a bigger risk to take on.

◆ Think about the doubts that the interviewer has about you at your stage of your career.

◆ Rehearse some answers for the sort of questions that the interviewer could ask you.

8

Coping with other Types of Interview

In this Chapter . . .

- ◆ Common variations on the basic interview
- ◆ Estimating market sizes
- ◆ Mastering case study interviews
- ◆ Example case study problems
- ◆ Handling brainteasers
- ◆ What else can employers throw at you?

So far, I have covered the sorts of questions that you might face in conventional job interviews. Most of the time, you the candidate will be asked questions about your skills, qualities and experience, by a single interviewer in an office environment. However, there are many alternatives to the traditional interview, some of which are more prevalent in certain industries or sectors, that you need to be prepared for.

If the employer is likely to use any of these other interview formats, you should be able to find out beforehand. When telephoning ahead to check the time, date and location of the interview, ask questions such as: "How long is the interview going to take?" and "Will there just be the one interviewer?" In most cases, you will be told if there is more than one interviewer or an unusual interview format.

INTERVIEWS ARE NOT ALWAYS ONE ON ONE

There may be many interviewers facing you, or there may be a number of other candidates being interviewed at the same time. Each different situation has its own unique challenges.

Panel interviews

Panel interviews are particularly popular in the public sector, where it is not uncommon to be faced with a row of six or seven (or even more) interviewers.

When faced with so many interviewers, you will have little chance to work on building a rapport with them. In such situations, try to:

◆ **Build what little rapport you can** by introducing yourself to each of the interviewers on the panel. A simple hand-shake and hello to each person in turn should be acceptable to even the stuffiest of panels.

◆ **Maintain eye contact with the person on the panel who asks you each question**. However, do also look occasionally at the other people on the panel.

◆ **Take your time to think before you answer each question**. With so many interviewers – each of who has their own agenda and line of questioning – it would be easy to get confused by the interrogative nature of the panel interview.

◆ **Take no notice of note takers**. There may be people on the panel whose job it is to take notes continuously, or each interviewer may just take notes for themselves. In either case, try not to be distracted by how little, or how much, they are writing.

Multiple interviews

A variation on having many people interview you at the same time is to have them interview you one after another. You might find yourself having three or four interviews of maybe only half-an-hour, or an hour each.

When you do find yourself faced with several people, possibly asking you the same questions, don't be afraid to use the same examples in answering the same questions. However, if you do use the same examples, make sure that you are consistent each time, as the interviewers may compare details afterwards and look for any discrepancies in what they have each heard.

Also try to find out the job title of each interviewer. Most interviewers open an interview by telling you their job title and a little bit about their background, but they can forget to do so. So do ask. Once you have established their job title, you will have a better idea of what each particular interviewer's interests and concerns might be. For example, an interviewer from marketing may be looking for innovation and creative ideas, while an interviewer with a finance background may be more interested in the extent to which you can operate within tight budgets.

Group interviews

Group interviews are not the same as group discussions (which are covered in Chapter 9). Group interviews are often used in the airline industry to reduce the many applicants to a more manageable number that they will then subject to more personalised interviewing.

The interviewers may invite volunteers to stand up and introduce themselves to the interviewers and the rest of the group, or they may ask only two or three questions for each of the candidates to answer in turn.

The interviewers are looking for enthusiasm and confidence in a group situation. They are trying to eliminate candidates who clearly do not have sufficient interpersonal skills. So make sure that you:

◆ Are always one of the first few candidates to volunteer for anything. Candidates who are late to volunteer are unlikely to be taken through to further rounds of the interviewing process.
◆ Speak in a clear and loud enough voice for everyone to hear.
◆ Smile and try to appear relaxed but enthusiastic.
◆ Try to distinguish yourself from the crowd. For example, have something interesting to say if they ask: "Tell us something about yourself that no one else in the room knows." Or prepare a joke in case they should ask for one.

Agency/headhunter/executive search firm interviews

There are many intermediary companies that can act on

behalf of employers. Sometimes it is possible to approach agencies or recruitment consultants. Occasionally, the telephone may ring and a headhunter may have an offer for you.

In both cases, they may ask you to meet with them to discuss the types of role you are looking for or perhaps a particular vacancy on offer. Some tips:

◆ Despite being couched as an 'informal conversation', it is still an interview. Dress the part and prepare accordingly to answer the full range of questions that you might expect to be asked at any formal employer interview.

◆ Remember that the agency is paid by the employer – they are seeking to meet the needs of the client first and foremost. Even though they may appear to be very supportive, they are likely to be screening multiple candidates. So do not take enthusiasm on their part as a guarantee that they will ultimately put you in front of any of their client employers.

◆ Use the agency as an opportunity to gain interview practice. The agency may suggest that you interview with some employers that you might (secretly) not be very interested in. However, go along to the interview anyway. It will help you to practise for the job interviews that you do eventually want to get.

If you are eventually offered a role with an employer through an agency, make sure that you do your own research to find out whether the employer organisation's culture and the nature of the role fit your particular needs. Many agencies get a final fee for placing a candidate, and some unscrupulous agencies may oversell the role – perhaps focusing only on the positive aspects of the job and making it sound more exciting than it might be – to get you to accept it and allow them to receive their final commission. So be aware of such pressures and make up your own mind.

PROFESSIONAL SERVICES FIRMS LIKE TO ASK CANDIDATES TO ESTIMATE

Management consultancies and investment banks, in particular, like to use case study interviews. Typical questions might ask you to estimate the size of a market, for example: "How many mobile phones are there in China?" or "How many litres of orange juice are consumed in France each year?"

On the face of it, these would seem impossible to answer, as you are not going to have the facts to hand. However, the interviewer is actually interested in two key skills:

1. Your capacity to make estimates, apply rules of thumb, and extrapolate from information that you do possess, when no definitive data is available.
2. How quickly you can make mental calculations.

The interviewer is not expecting you to have the actual answers. In fact, behind closed doors, the interviewers often talk about case studies as testing candidates' abilities to "guesstimate" answers to questions. They are more interested in hearing your thought processes on tackling the question. So one critical tip (which the interviewers often forget to mention) is to *talk aloud as you work out the answer to the problem.*

Here is a sample question along with a candidate's response:

How many cars are there in Australia?

Start by breaking down the question into the facts that you would need to estimate. For example, in order to estimate the answer, you need to know how many people are in Australia. Then you would need to figure out the ratio of people to cars in the country. A candidate's answer might go along the lines of the following:

"I have no idea of the exact population of Australia. I know that it is a huge country, but it is much less densely populated than most European countries. I know that the population of the UK is less than 60 million people, so perhaps Australia has 20 million inhabitants – give or take a few million?

"Now, not everyone has a car. People may live in family units – so even though there may be 20 million people living in Australia, we probably only have about 7 million households, because on average maybe three people live in each household. Not every household has a car though, so let's say that only one in two households has a car. Obviously, some households have more than one car – but there are lots of people who travel only on public transport. So of the 7 million households, I'd say there were about 3.5 million cars in Australia."

Now, your estimates may have a significant margin of error attached to them. But as long as they are sensible and not completely ridiculous – you can demonstrate your ability to break a problem down and make rapid mental calculations.

INTERVIEWERS MAY ALSO ASK YOU TO ANALYSE PROBLEMS

Professional services firms may also ask candidates to analyse problems and suggest solutions – pretending, for example, that you had been posed a question by a client who is willing to pay you for your consultancy advice.

In such a situation, the interviewer is looking for your ability to:

◆ Apply logic to break a complex problem into a number of more easily solved component problems.
◆ Gather and analyse information.
◆ Make suggestions while thinking on your feet.

Again, you are expected to talk the interviewer through your chain of logic and ask questions of the interviewer, so make sure that you:

◆ Listen carefully to the question. If the question involves multiple points and sub-questions, ask whether the interviewer would mind you jotting down some of the key points on a sheet of paper to act as a reminder.
◆ Ask whether you are allowed to ask the interviewer questions along the way or whether you are expected to work the answer out on your own.

TWO EXAMPLE CASE STUDY PROBLEMS

The following are examples of the sorts of questions that you might be asked. However, the depth of your analysis and precise level of detail that you need to provide will vary according to the seniority of the role that you are being interviewed for. An undergraduate, for example, might be expected to be less detailed than a senior manager with an MBA under her belt.

Why are supermarket own-brand cans of baked beans cheaper than the leading make of branded baked beans?

No technical knowledge about food production is actually needed to answer the question as this question is trying to ascertain the candidate's ability to make sensible assumptions and to break down an initially complicated-seeming problem. A candidate's answer might go as follows:

"Well, I assume that own-brand baked beans are cheaper because they cost less to produce. So why don't we break down the cost of different cans of beans into their constituent parts.

"Thinking about the constituent parts, there are the basic costs of the beans themselves. Perhaps the branded company can buy beans in more cheaply, because they buy in bigger quantities and can get them in bulk. The branded beans company would also probably be able to buy in tin cans more cheaply, again because they buy in greater quantities. However, those two facts would suggest that the branded beans should be cheaper – so that's not the answer.

"Another part of the cost is the distribution of the tins of beans – but I can't see why there would be a significant difference in cost there either. Aha! – I've got it. Supermarkets never advertise their baked beans on the television, whereas the branded company has to spend much more on marketing and advertising, so that's why supermarkets can sell their beans more cheaply.''

There is the answer. So remember that succeeding at case study interviews is about breaking down a problem, and then making some quick estimates and mental calculations.

Let's think about an imaginary company called Goops. This company is the UK's leading health and beauty product retailer with 200 stores in the UK. Its revenues and profits have increased year on year for the last ten years. However, a large European competitor has just bought up the numbers two and four health and beauty retailers in the UK. The Chief Executive of Goops has called you in for advice. What would you suggest?

The following represents the dialogue between the interviewer (I) and the candidate (C):

C: Firstly, I'd like to get some more information on the situation. I hope you won't mind if I write some of this down?

I: No, go ahead.

C: Okay. You say that the European competitor has bought up the numbers two and four retailers. What do you mean by numbers two and four? Are these ranked by revenue or profits or something else?

I: The rankings are based on numbers of stores.

C: Okay, so how many stores do these two retailers each have?

I: The number two retailer has 160 stores and the number four has 70 stores.

C: And does the European competitor have any of its own stores in the UK?

I: No, it doesn't. Buying these two retailers is its first venture into the UK.

C: Now I'd like to understand whether the second and fourth largest retailers actually compete in the same market as Goops. Do they have a similar product mix?

I: Yes. None of the three retailers manufactures their own products – they rely completely on products made by their suppliers.

C: What about their prices? Do they have the same price points?

I: Some products may be cheaper in one store than another, but their average prices are roughly similar.

C: Do the three retailers compete in roughly the same geographic areas?

I: Yes. They all tend to cluster on the high streets of larger towns and cities. So you may even see them next door to each other at times.

C: Well, it sounds like by combining numbers two and four, this European business will become bigger than Goops and be able to have greater economies of scale and be able to drive down prices and gain market share. Hang on. How big is the number three competitor in this segment?

I: The number three has 85 stores. And it is owned by a struggling American company, which has publicly stated that it wants to divest its overseas holdings to focus on its core North American stores.

C: Ah, so they might be willing to sell to Goops?

I: Possibly.

C: Well, on the face of it, it looks as if Goops might want
        to think about raising funds to buy the third player in
        the market. Then they would have nearly 300 stores
        and continue to be the number one player. However, I
        would want to do a lot more analysis to understand
        whether this suggestion would work.

I: That sounds like a good idea. Well done.

BRAINTEASERS TEST YOUR ABILITY TO THINK LATERALLY

Some interviewers like to pose riddles, quandaries, or brainteasers to test candidates' ability to 'think out of the box'.
These are unlikely to have a right or wrong answer – in fact
there may be many possible solutions. The only tip here is to
let your imagination run wild.

Let's consider an example:

**You are in a room with three light switches, each of
which controls one of three light bulbs in an adjacent
room. You must determine which switch controls which
bulb. But I'm afraid there are some constraints – you may
only flick two switches and may enter the adjacent room
only once. How would you go about determining which
switch controls which bulb?**

There are a number of ways you could solve the puzzle. The
best way is to flick one switch on, wait for five minutes and
flick it back off. Then turn one of the other light switches on
before going into the room. This allows you to work out
which switch controls which light. By feeling which light bulb

feels warm, you can identify which switch controlled it. And then the other two are easy enough to work out.

Alternative solutions could include:

◆ Knocking a hole in the wall so that you could see which switch controls which bulb.
◆ Asking a friend to enter the room so that you can ask which bulb comes on.
◆ Asking the interviewer whether there is a window in the door that you can look through.
◆ Buying a mirror and placing it strategically so that you can see which bulbs are operated by which switches.
◆ And so on.

As you can see, there may be many possible responses to brainteasers such as these. If one stumps you, don't discount any answer at all. Answers that appear silly to you could be acceptable to the interviewer.

INTERVIEWS CAN HAPPEN IN UNUSUAL SITUATIONS AND VENUES

Although the majority of interviews are conducted in office surroundings, some are not.

Telephone interviews

A few companies like to screen candidates over the tele-phone before inviting them to interview. The interviewer is usually looking to check your qualifications or experience. As such the questions are likely to be more straightforward.

This is a difficult situation as there is little opportunity to establish a rapport with the interviewer, especially without visual clues as to whether the interviewer is bored or interested in what you are saying. However, resist the urge to be too pushy or to speak for too long. Your aim is to be invited to a face-to-face interview, as opposed to arguing why you are better than the other candidates and should be offered the job.

Many candidates feel more nervous being questioned over the telephone, but the following tips may help you to make a better impression on the interviewer:

◆ Have copies of your CV and any other written materials in front of you. It may also help you to jot down beforehand some bullet point answers to the more likely questions that you may be asked – this will reduce the risk of forgetting to mention any key points about yourself or your experience.

◆ Stand up while you speak on the telephone. Most people find that they sound more confident on the telephone as a result.

◆ Smile down the telephone. Even though the interviewer cannot see you, people typically report that it helps to put them into a more relaxed frame of mind and sound friendlier.

Touch-tone telephone quizzes

A few companies have started asking candidates to listen to multiple-choice questions on the telephone that they must respond to, by pressing keys on their touch-tone telephones.

For example, you might be asked questions such as: "Which option would you choose? Imagine that you have spotted a colleague stealing some blank computer disks from the store cupboard. Press key number 1 if you would stop her and ask her what she is doing. Press number 2 if you would report the incident to your boss. Press 3 if you would report it to personnel. Or press 4 if you would ignore the incident."

If you are asked by a potential employer to participate in such a quiz:

◆ Ask the person you are speaking to for as much information as possible. How long will the quiz take? What sorts of questions will you be asked? What keys should you press if you are confused by the options or have made a mistake?

◆ Listen carefully during the quiz. Make sure that you are in a quiet room with no risk of being disturbed.

◆ Have a pen and paper in front of you so that you can take notes if you need to.

Interviews over food

An interview over breakfast, lunch or dinner may be sold to you as an informal opportunity for you to find out about the company as well as vice versa. But make no mistake that you are being formally evaluated as much as if you were being questioned in an office environment.

Some tips for handling meal etiquette:

◆ Always follow the lead of your interviewer. Before ordering, ask the interviewer if he or she is having just a main course, or a starter and main. You do not want to establish a reputation for gluttony.

◆ Avoid the most expensive items even though they may be the most appetising.

◆ Choose a dish that is easy to eat while talking. Spaghetti is a nightmare to eat without mess or fuss.

◆ Steer clear of alcohol, even if the interviewer is having a drink. You need to keep your wits about you. If the interviewer insists, then ask for some water as well as alcohol, and nurse your drink slowly.

◆ Avoid smoking. In an increasingly anti-smoking age, you may as well admit that you are a murderer. If you must have a cigarette, then do it away from the table.

SUMMARY

◆ Telephone ahead to check the style and number of interviews that you may be faced with.

◆ Talk aloud when estimating market sizes or solving case study problems. The interviewer is as interested in your thought processes as the final answer.

◆ Think imaginatively when posed brainteasers. There may be many acceptable answers as opposed to a single 'right' answer.

◆ Spread out your CV and notes for easy access, before participating in a telephone interview.

◆ Be the perfect guest when invited to interview over food. Eat and drink only as much as the interviewer.

9

Succeeding at Assessment Centres

In this Chapter . . .

- ◆ Dealing with in-tray exercises
- ◆ Passing psychometric tests
- ◆ Giving presentations
- ◆ Contributing to group exercises
- ◆ Handling role play simulations

Assessment centres are an increasingly popular way for employers to assess the skills of candidates. Rather than simply asking candidates to talk about their skills, the interviewers want to observe those skills in action.

Assessment centres have been popular with employers for selecting graduates. However, they are increasingly being used for managerial levels and for purposes of internal promotion.

The term 'assessment centre' does not necessarily refer to a special building or location. It simply refers to an approach that combines a variety of different methods such as in-tray exercises, role play simulations, presentations, and psychometric tests to provide a more thorough picture of the strengths and weaknesses of candidates. You could be assessed on your own or in a group with other candidates. You could be assessed for only a few hours or up to several days.

One reason why employers use assessment centres is that they are harder to fake than interviews. The scenarios and situations that you face will vary greatly from one employer to the next. However, this chapter covers general pointers and tips that should help you perform at your best.

IN-TRAY EXERCISES

In-tray exercises try to simulate the typical demands that you might face on your desk if you were to be successful in joining the company. You might be presented with a pile of memos, faxes, reports and other correspondence requiring your attention.

For example, the instructions may start: "It's Monday today, the first day in your new job. It is 9 a.m. and you have taken over from the previous manager who left only last Friday. Unfortunately, he did not clear his desk before leaving the company, therefore it is up to you to deal with all of his remaining correspondence."

You may be asked to read the documents and respond in writing to the most important. For example: "In order to deal with the correspondence in the in-tray, you may choose to write, type or telephone your responses. You have been provided with blank memo pro formas to write on. There is a computer for you to type emails, or you may choose to use the telephone to leave voicemails for colleagues."

Managing in-tray exercises

In-tray exercises are usually timed so that you will not be able to read all of the information in detail. Most in-trays contain both critical information as well as secondary information that is designed to distract you from the more critical items.

If you believe that you may be faced with an in-tray exercise, you may want to take along some of the usual stationery that you would have access to in your own office. For example, if coloured pens and Post-It notes would help you to prioritise items, then make sure that you have a supply of these in your briefcase.

Then do read the instructions carefully as different in-trays will require you to respond in different ways.

Graduate in-trays

Graduate in-trays or in-trays aimed at junior managers often test the ability to prioritise and organise work. They often ask you to respond to each and every item within the in-tray.

As such, you should skim-read all of the information and sort out all of the materials into one of three piles:

◆ *Urgent information* that is both important and needs acting upon immediately. For example, a complaint from a key customer may need sorting out as quickly as possible.

◆ *Important information* that needs your attention, but only when you have sorted through all of the most urgent items. For example, there may be a complaint from a smaller customer, which you would need to answer once you had answered the complaint from the key customer.

◆ *Non-urgent information* that could wait until a later date for you to deal with it. For example, there may be memos from senior managers that need your response at some point – but not today.

When you have sorted your initial information into the three piles, you should begin by tackling the urgent items. The instructions for the in-tray exercise should explain exactly what you should do. Perhaps you need to write a memo or type an email to deal with the item. Work through all of the urgent items before starting on the important ones. If you finish all the important items, then you could start the non-urgent items – but only then.

Frequently, there may be additional information given to you at intervals throughout the day. Interviewers like to see how you deal with interruptions. When the new material arrives, just deal with it in the same way, by prioritising it into the above three piles.

Senior manager in-trays

In-trays are quite common as part of internal promotion assessment centres, but are gaining greater acceptance for the recruitment of senior external candidates as well.

In-trays at this level usually require a more strategic approach. The assessors are looking for the ability to balance the need to deal with important short-term issues as well as important long-term issues.

For example, an in-tray might ask you to identify:

1. Short-term, urgent issues that must be dealt with in the next two to three days.
2. Medium-term issues that must be dealt with over the next four months, by the end of the business year.
3. Issues that affect the long-term (12+ months) viability of the organisation.

If the instructions ask you to spend time on two or three separate tasks, try to allocate time to all of them rather than finishing one off completely and neglecting the others. It is better to give some evidence that you are able to be both strategic and tactical at the same time rather than giving evidence that you are only able to do one or the other.

PSYCHOMETRIC TESTS NEED NOT BE AT ALL INTIMIDATING

Many candidates fear the prospect of being subjected to psychometric tests. But there is no need to be afraid if you understand their purpose. There are actually two distinct categories of psychometric tests:

1. Aptitude tests, which measure skills and abilities. Aptitude tests do have right or wrong answers.
2. Personality inventories, which measure preferences

and motivations. These try to measure how you generally like to behave in certain situations. What do you like or dislike? These do not have right or wrong answers, although the employer may be looking for candidates who have a certain 'type' of personality.

Aptitude tests

Aptitude tests are frequently used as a predictor of on-the-job performance. They are often also called 'ability tests' or 'cognitive tests'. Most commonly, these are used to measure numeracy or verbal reasoning skills. However, for technical jobs, employers may also try to assess skills such as spatial reasoning or abstract reasoning. Speed and accuracy are essential, so make sure that you:

- *Read the instructions thoroughly.* Most of the errors made by candidates are made because they did not read the instructions carefully enough. Take note of any unusual directions. For example, one test might ask you to put a pen tick in a box for the answer that you think is right, whereas another test might ask you to completely fill in a circle using pencil.
- *Identify how the scoring works.* For example, some aptitude tests take marks off if you make mistakes, so it may be worth working slowly but accurately. Other tests simply add on marks for each question that you did correctly – so it may be worth guessing the answers to a few questions if you are running out of time.
- *Keep an eye on the time.* Most aptitude tests are timed. It may be worth doing a quick mental calculation to see how long you should spend on each question. For example, if there are 60 questions in total to be

completed in 45 minutes, then if you struggle with any question for more than a minute, you should definitely move on. If you do not usually wear a watch, it may be worth borrowing one or taking a small timer along with you to an interview in case the employer should spring an aptitude test on you.

Aptitude tests are designed to be difficult, so try not to worry too much about questions that you do not understand and are forced to skip. Most employers specifically design their aptitude tests so that average candidates will be allowed to make maybe several dozen mistakes and still pass the test. Even the brightest and best candidates will still make a few mistakes.

Personality questionnaires

Personality questionnaires can take many different shapes and forms. The majority are still presented to you as pencil-and-paper questions for you to read through and respond to. However, a few companies have adopted computerised testing, which asks you simply to type your responses.

Some questionnaires ask you to answer yes/no to a number of questions. Others may ask you to respond whether you 'strongly agree', 'agree', 'disagree' or 'strongly disagree' with a series of statements. Some may ask you to write your answers directly on the question book, while others may ask you to circle your answers on a separate answer sheet. So the first tip is to *read the instructions carefully* to make sure that you are not making a fool of yourself.

The second tip is to *be very careful of trying to second-guess personality questionnaires*. Different personality question-naires measure different dimensions of personality and it may be very difficult to know exactly what the interviewers are looking for. For example, you might assume that a particular job requires employees who are very extrovert. But this employer might have looked at previous employees and discovered in their research that the extremely extrovert employees tend to get bored and leave quickly. So the interviewers may in fact prefer employees who are less extrovert. You cannot tell what the 'right' answer may be. Consequently, you may distort your responses in the wrong direction. Giving responses that you think the interviewer is looking for could ruin your chances of getting the job.

Guessing what to put down is fraught with difficulties, so honesty really is the best policy. Another tip to help you is to *read each statement or question once and write down the first honest answer that comes into your head*. Better to put down your gut response than agonise over a response to put down.

Finally, the British Psychological Society recommends that employers should give feedback to candidates on the results of any personality questionnaires. The feedback may be a written report or simply a few minutes of debriefing over the telephone. However, not all employers do so automatically – so you may need to ask.

Going online

There are a number of aptitude and personality inventories that you can practise completing for free. Practice can help to improve your scores on aptitude tests and alleviate any anxiety about completing personality questionnaires.

The following are some of the better websites that you might like to start with:

◆ www.money.guardian.co.uk/work – the *Guardian* newspaper has a series of short aptitude tests that you can try out online.
◆ www.morrisby.com – this website has a section for test takers, which contains nine pages of aptitude tests including questions on mechanical ability and abstract reasoning.
◆ www.shldirect.com – this is the website of a large test publisher. It has examples of a variety of verbal, numeric and diagrammatic reasoning test questions, as well as sample questions from a personality questionnaire.
◆ www.ase-solutions.co.uk/support.asp – another website of a large test publisher. This gives you the opportunity to practise verbal and numerical reasoning as well as emotional intelligence questions.

Many university careers service websites also have test-taking practice questions. Use your favourite search engine to track these down.

THE SECRET OF GOOD PRESENTATIONS IS PREPARATION

Increasingly, employers are looking for candidates with good oral communication and presentation skills. Some employers ask candidates to prepare a presentation beforehand, while others prefer to give candidates a topic to present on during the day of the assessment centre itself.

You can improve your performance during presentations by preparing in the following ways:

◆ *Structure your presentation*. There is an adage that says 'tell the audience what you are going to say, then say it, then remind them what you said'. Begin with a short introduction to the topic before the main body of your presentation. End with a short summary of the key points of the presentation.

◆ *Use simple visual aids*. Candidates who choose simply to speak without visual aids can be quite boring to watch. Visual aids provide something else for the audience to focus on. It will also help to prompt you.

◆ *Use bullet points as opposed to large tracts of text*. Visual aids should be clear and uncluttered. If appropriate, any charts, graphs or simple diagrams will also help to prevent monotony.

◆ *Choose straightforward visual aids*. If you have a choice, use either flip charts and coloured pens or overhead transparencies. The assessors are trying to evaluate your confidence and style of presentation – not your technical know-how, so why risk using high-tech solutions such as slide projectors or computer software such as PowerPoint that are far more likely to go wrong?

◆ *Watch the time*. Your instructions will give you strict instructions on your allotted time – so make sure that you stick to it. Also read the instructions carefully to see if you are expected to leave time to invite questions from the audience as well.

GROUP EXERCISES ARE GOVERNED BY A FEW SIMPLE RULES

Group exercises are often included in assessment centres – particularly those at graduate level. However, they are also popular for internal promotion processes – for example: when middle managers are being considered for the jump into senior management.

Such exercises typically involve between four and ten participants. The group could be made up entirely of other candidates for the job, or may comprise some candidates and some assessors.

Group exercises are impossible to predict beforehand. Some group exercises may ask candidates to complete a task. For example, there may be a business plan for a fictitious company along with instructions for the group to evaluate the plan and make recommendations on how the business should proceed. Or the task may appear slightly frivolous – such as constructing a tower out of children's play bricks. However, the majority of group exercises simply invite candidates to discuss a particular theme or issue and reach a consensus of opinion by the end of the discussion.

Because group exercises do vary enormously, you will not be able to prepare what you say. But you can think about how you behave towards others, as group exercises are often an opportunity to evaluate how well you can work as part of a team.

Tips for handling group exercises

If you are faced with a group exercise, make sure that you:

◆ *Avoid dominating the discussion.* Give others an opportunity to speak and avoid interrupting them until they have finished.

◆ *Watch your body language.* It can be easy to drift off when other people are speaking. At least look as if you are paying attention.

◆ *Never dismiss anyone else's ideas.* No matter how stupid another person's point of view, try to say something that acknowledges their contribution and perhaps get someone else in the group to disagree with them on your behalf – "That's a valid point of view. But does anyone else have a different view?"

◆ *Avoid jumping to conclusions.* You may have slightly different information from the other candidates. It is not uncommon for each candidate to be given one or two pieces of information that no one else has. So check whether this is the case before making any decisions.

◆ *Always criticise constructively.* If you must disagree, try to build on what has been said previously, rather than suggest something completely new.

◆ *Involve the quieter members of the group.* For example, if you notice that one person is particularly quiet, you could use their name and ask what they think – "I'm not trying to pick on you, Maeve, but I just want to make sure that you are happy with what's being said?"

ROLE PLAY SIMULATIONS TEST YOUR ABILITY TO LISTEN

Role play simulations allow employers to observe how you *actually* behave, as opposed to how you say you would behave in a given situation. Typically, you will be given time to read some instructions before interacting with a trained actor or an assessor. You might even interact with a number of actors or assessors.

These simulations try to mimic the situations that you might face if you worked for the employer. For example, you might be told that a colleague has called in sick and be asked to step in on her behalf to deal with an irate customer, or you might be expected to mediate a dispute between two colleagues. A managerial role play scenario could ask you to discipline a troublesome member of the team. The options are nearly endless.

Typically, candidates are given preparation time along with written instructions and background materials to read before meeting the assessor. During your preparation time, you should:

◆ *Read the instructions carefully*. Note how much preparation time you have and the time you will have for the role play.

◆ *Make a list of questions that you want to ask*. The background materials may portray a situation that seems very black and white. You may seem right and the other person may seem to be in the wrong. However, the assessor or actor may possess information in their heads that you do not have – perhaps you are actually the one who has been deliberately misinformed by the instructions. So it is worth checking what they do or do not know.

◆ *Write down any objectives that you have*. For example, if there are five key points that you want to discuss with the assessor, you can tick these off when you actually come to the meeting.

General tips for role plays

Whatever the scenario, the following tips will help you to succeed at role plays:

◆ *Treat it seriously.* Role play simulations can sometimes seem a bit artificial – both you and the assessor know that this is not real life. But you should treat the situation as if it were real life. Being flippant or acting 'out of role' will do you no favours.

◆ *Build a rapport with the assessor.* The temptation on first meeting the assessor or actor might be to jump in with the main task that you have been given. But it usually makes sense to spend just a few minutes exchanging pleasantries, as you would do with any person that you are meeting for the first time.

◆ *Seek compromises.* Avoid charging into a role play simulation with a plan of action that you will stick to regardless. Seek a middle ground whenever you can.

◆ *Be balanced in giving feedback.* Quite often, role play simulations may require you to discipline a difficult team member. Many candidates fall into the trap of just delivering unpleasant, negative feedback. However, you should also look in the instructions and materials provided, to see if there is any positive feedback that you could also give the team member.

◆ *Stay calm.* Displaying anger or even a tiny flash of irritation is sure to harm your chances of getting the job. The assessors have been asked to behave in certain ways

– for example: to become angry with you or perhaps even cry. You should try to remain polite at all times.

SUMMARY

◆ Prioritise in-tray documents into urgent, important, and non-urgent piles. Then work systematically through the documents.

◆ Keep an eye on the time and work methodically through aptitude tests.

◆ Avoid second-guessing personality questionnaires.

◆ Help the other participants to get involved when you are involved in a group exercise.

◆ Ask questions, listen, and seek compromises in role play simulations.

10

Asking the Right Questions

In this Chapter . . .

◆ Preparing intelligent questions
◆ Exploring the nature of the work
◆ Asking about the future
◆ Finding out about the culture of the company
◆ Questions to avoid

At some point during the proceedings, the interviewer may ask: "Do you have any questions?" It is then over to you, to provide the questions.

Interviewers frequently judge candidates on the nature of the questions that are asked. Do you ask about the pay and benefits? Are you focused about the day-to-day demands of the role? Or are you more interested about opportunities for promotion and enhanced responsibility? Different questions give interviewers different impressions about your motivations.

However, do not forget that this is your opportunity to find more out about the job and the company. If the interviewer were to offer you the job, would you have enough information to decide whether to accept it or not?

This chapter contains many examples of questions for you to tailor to different interviewers and employers that you may meet. Not all of them will be appropriate for every situation, so think ahead and choose carefully.

ASK DIFFERENT QUESTIONS IN EACH AND EVERY INTERVIEW

Intelligent and thoughtful questions can demonstrate to an interviewer that you had the motivation and interest to do your research on the organisation. However, when preparing a list of questions to ask your prospective employer, make sure that your questions could not have been answered in any other way. Many companies provide information in recruitment brochures, websites, job descriptions and other materials as well as the original job advert. If you ask a question that could have been answered in any of these other sources of information, you could come across as poorly prepared.

For example, it may be a valid question to ask Company A about their plans for international expansion – however, Company B may have published a lengthy statement about their expansion plans on their website. Accordingly, **be careful that your questions are relevant for the particular company that you are being interviewed by**. If you simply take the same list of questions to different interviewers, you risk ruining your chances.

Your research may uncover dozens and dozens of questions that you might want to ask. However, asking too many questions could annoy your interviewer – especially if he or she has arranged to interview a number of candidates and is running behind schedule. Here are some rules of thumb for asking questions:

◆ Ask at least two or three questions to show that you have done your research and are interested in finding more about the company.

◆ Avoid asking more than half-a-dozen questions during the interview itself. Should you be offered the job, you could always arrange to come back to meet the interviewer or other people within the organisation, to have your questions answered.

SHOW AN INTEREST IN YOUR ROLE

There are many questions that you could ask about the role. However, remember to check that the questions you do choose to ask could not have been answered in your research.

Questions to ask could include:

◆ "What are the day-to-day duties involved in this job?"
◆ "How will my performance be measured?"
◆ "How are targets set? How much say would I have in setting them?"
◆ "Who will I report to?"
◆ "Who would I be spending most of my working time with?"

♦ "Who are the key decision makers that I would need to get along with, and how would you describe each of them?"

♦ "What sort of budget would I have for running the team?"

♦ "What do you see as the immediate challenges for me if I were to be given the job?"

You might also want to find out more about why the employer is looking to fill this role:

♦ "Why has this vacancy arisen?"

♦ "What happened to the previous job holder?"

♦ "Are you looking for anything in particular from the person who will take this role?"

♦ "How do you see this role developing?"

♦ "How quickly are you looking for someone to take on this role?"

Questions about the company

You could also ask questions about the structure and current challenges facing the company as a whole:

♦ "How is the department that I would be joining viewed by the rest of the organisation?"

♦ "How is the company structured?"

♦ "When was the last company restructuring, and how did it affect this department?"

♦ "What challenges is the organisation currently facing?"

Or, if you have an insight into how the company is perceived against its competitors, these could also be good questions to ask, as it can show off the research that you have done. For example: "I read in the papers that your competitor, Company X, has just launched a new service line. What's the view in your company on it, and how are you going to react to it?"

DEMONSTRATE YOUR INTEREST IN HAVING A FUTURE WITH THE EMPLOYER

I have already mentioned the fact that employers usually want to recruit employees who will stay for at least two to three years. So it may be worth your while to ask some questions about the future.

For example, you could ask about your own future with the company:

◆ "What training and development is given to employees?"
◆ "What opportunities are there for promotion?"
◆ "What opportunities are there for working abroad with the company?"
◆ "How does the company promote personal growth?"

Questions about the company

You might also want to ask about the company's prospects:

◆ "What are the company's long-term objectives?"
◆ "How has the company been performing in recent months?"
◆ "What are the company's plans for growth, and how will it achieve these?"
◆ "What new products/services is the company planning to launch?"

◆ "Are any organisational changes planned in the near future?"

DON'T FORGET TO ASK ABOUT THE COMPANY CULTURE

No matter how informative the website and other official sources of information, you need to be able to talk to people about the culture – the way in which people behave towards one another on a day-to-day basis.

Some general questions to ask:

◆ "How would you describe the culture of the organisation?"
◆ "What's the best thing about working for this organisation?"
◆ "What most frustrates you about working here?"
◆ "How would you describe the management style around here?"
◆ "What does it take to succeed around here?"
◆ "Could you tell me about the sorts of people who have failed here? What was it they did or didn't do that made them unsuccessful?"

Or you could use questions to probe on more specific issues:

◆ "Would you describe this as a political organisation? And if so, why?"
◆ "Is there much inter-departmental rivalry in the company?"
◆ "How would you describe the company's attitude to risk taking?"

- "How does the company respond to new threats and opportunities?"
- "How much autonomy and latitude are people given in the organisation?"
- "How much do people socialise together outside work?"

AVOID CERTAIN QUESTIONS UNTIL YOU HAVE AN OFFER ON THE TABLE

There may be certain burning questions that you really want to ask and have answered, but you do not want to risk leaving the interviewer with the wrong sort of impression. So it may be better to avoid certain areas of discussion until you have a firm job offer.

Topics to stay away from therefore include:

- Pay, benefits and annual leave allowances.
- Criteria and processes for being awarded pay rises.
- Flexible working practices such as working from home or maternity/paternity leave.
- The workload and length of the working day.

SUMMARY

- Prepare a list of questions to ask of your interviewer.

- Check that none of your questions could have been answered by any source other than asking the interviewer.

- Focus most of your questions on the role and responsibilities of the job.

◆ Use your questions to check that the culture of the organisation would suit you.

◆ Steer clear of questions on money and other topics that could make you appear greedy or lazy.

11

Ending on a High Note

In this Chapter . . .

◆ Making a graceful exit
◆ Writing follow-up letters
◆ How can references make the difference?

By now you should have answered the interviewer's many questions and had the opportunity to ask a few of your own. You may think that there is little else you can do – but you would be wrong to think so.

LEAVE THE INTERVIEWER WITH A GOOD FINAL IMPRESSION

Experience tells us that first impressions matter. But psychologists have found that final impressions can also have a disproportionately large impact on how you will be remembered.

Some points to keep in mind as you prepare to leave:

◆ Check what the next steps will be. Is this the only interview? If not, when will they decide who to invite back to the second/third/etc rounds of interview?

◆ Make a final statement about your enthusiasm for the job. "I'd like to say that I really like what I've heard about the company. And I really look forward to being invited back for a second/third/etc interview."

◆ Finally, shake hands firmly with the interviewer, smile, and thank them for their time.

Dealing with spontaneous job offers

It is unlikely that you will be offered a job on the spot. In fact, you will probably not be offered a job there and then in 95% of cases.

However, in those 5% of cases where you may be in the final stage of an interview and perhaps the only remaining candidate, it can happen. If you do find yourself being offered a job at the end of an interview:

◆ Express your excitement to be offered the job. "That's fantastic – I'm very pleased because I like what I have heard about the role and company so far."

◆ Ask for time to think about the job offer. "I would like to accept the offer. But I want to make sure that I don't rush into a decision, so I'd like a few days to think about it."

◆ Ask for more detail about the offer – preferably in writing. "Would it be possible to send me a sample contract so that I can see what you are offering me?"

◆ Avoid accepting the offer. If you say yes now, you may be compromising your ability to negotiate a good package.

However, remember that it is unusual to be offered a job there and then. So do not be disappointed if the interviewer simply says good-bye.

FOLLOW-UP LETTERS SHOW YOUR ENTHUSIASM FOR THE JOB

Some candidates feel that writing a follow-up letter after an interview, like writing thank you letters for Christmas presents, is an old-fashioned practice. However, many interviewers *are* old-fashioned in their approach and appreciate the gesture. If your letter could influence the interviewer to choose you over another candidate, surely it is worth the effort?

As soon as you can, you should compose a short letter of no more than one page in length to the interviewer. Whether you send it in the post or by email, the key points to make in the letter are:

1. That you appreciated the interview and enjoyed meeting the interviewer

For example: "Thank you for making the time to see me. I very much enjoyed meeting you and having the opportunity to hear about the aggressive growth plans that the business has."

2. That you are enthusiastic about the job, the people, the challenge, or the company

For example: "The more I think about it, the more I believe that your plans for growth will make the business a very exciting place to be in over the next few years."

3. That you have the right skills and experience for the vacancy

Go on to recap in only one or two paragraphs what you believe those key skills and experiences are. For example: "I feel that my track record would make me an asset to your team. In particular, I have proven that I can deliver revenue growth quickly in the pharmaceuticals sector. Furthermore, I am sure that my work alongside external suppliers to implement change initiatives would also be of value."

4. That you would very much like to be invited back for the next round of interviews

"As such, I would very much like to be a part of the company. I realise that there is another round of interviews with the main board, and I would welcome the opportunity to convince them that I am the person for the job."

Or, if you had attended the final round of interviews, express how much you would like the job.

CHECK THAT YOUR REFERENCES ARE GOING TO BE POSITIVE

When making the final decision, the interviewer may choose to take into account your references. But it would be a shame for your references to let you down. Amazingly enough, some candidates ask former bosses and colleagues to write references for them without ensuring that those references will give them the best chance of getting the job as possible.

To ensure that your references will be suitably glowing, always write to your referees – perhaps just by email – to give them an idea of the key skills, experiences and qualities that you would like emphasised.

A sample letter to a referee

Dear Judy,

Thank you for agreeing to write a reference for me. As I explained on the telephone, I am applying to market research companies for a job as a researcher.

It would help me greatly if you could emphasise certain experiences from when I worked in your team:

◆ Account managing major clients such as Maximus Dog Foods and Parnassus TV Productions.
◆ Running focus groups and using quantitative surveys to evaluate brand impact of our clients' consumer goods.
◆ Presenting results back to clients.

I will give you a call in the next few days to see whether I can answer any other questions that you may have.

Best wishes,
Simon

After your referee has received your letter, you should ask whether he or she would mind giving you a draft of what they intend to say. And then, if you are asked by an interviewer to provide references, you can be confident of exactly what they will say about you.

SUMMARY

◆ Make a final statement about your enthusiasm for the job before you leave.

◆ Avoid accepting job offers on the spot as you could compromise your ability to negotiate the best package.

◆ Write a follow-up letter to remind the interviewer of your enthusiasm for the job.

◆ Brief your referees on what you would like them to say about you to potential employers.

12

Crossing the Finish Line

In this Chapter . . .

◆ Why take notes after the interview?
◆ Coping with rejection
◆ Reviewing your performance
◆ Asking for feedback
◆ Negotiating your package
◆ Accepting a job offer

The final interview is not the end of the interview *process*. If you were unsuccessful, you will need to review your performance and gather feedback to maximise your chances of securing the next job that you interview for.

Even if you were successful, there is still a little more work to come. Now that the employer has told you that they want to hire you, what would you like from them in terms of pay and package?

TAKING NOTES WILL HELP YOU JUGGLE JOB OFFERS

The reality of job hunting is that you may be applying to many firms and having interviews with several of them over quite a stretch of time. Unless you take notes, you may find it difficult to remember what you did or did not like about each company – which could make it difficult to decide which job offer to accept.

Note taking need not be laborious. What you write down is up to you. But many candidates find it useful to capture the following information:

◆ Name, address and telephone number of organisation.
◆ Name of interviewer(s).
◆ Date of interview(s) and when you expect to hear back from them – so that you can chase them if they have not got back to you when they said they would.
◆ What you liked about the company.
◆ What you did not like about the company.

This could be as little as a single sheet of A4 with some hand-scribbled notes. But as the weeks and months of interviewing pass, it will help to jog your memory when you need to take important decisions.

EVEN THE BEST CANDIDATES GET KNOCKED BACK OCCASIONALLY

It is natural to feel disappointed, angry or resentful not to get a job. But there can be all sorts of reasons for you not to get the offer. You may not have done anything wrong at all. The job may have gone to another candidate who had better skills and experience. Or the job may have gone to a favoured internal candidate.

On the other hand, perhaps you could have performed

better during the interview. Maybe you could have prepared your responses and examples more thoroughly. Or perhaps you should have focused more on building a rapport with the interviewer.

Whatever the reasons, don't let it get you down. Take an evening off and do something that you really enjoy. Forget about the job hunt for a while and let your hair down. Come back to the interview process refreshed. So long as you learn from each interview that you go to, you will get better and eventually get the job that is right for you.

HOW WELL DO YOU REALLY THINK YOUR INTERVIEW WENT?

Whether you were offered the job or not, it is a good idea to think about how well the interview went. If you were successful, it is still worth figuring out exactly what you did right that helped you to land the job.

Firstly, take a few minutes to ask yourself the following questions:

◆ *What went well?* What were you pleased with?
◆ *What went badly?* What would you do differently if you could do that interview all over again? Were you asked any questions that you did not have a good answer for?
◆ *What have you learned?* What can you apply to future interviews?

Don't move on until you have jotted down some thoughts to each of these questions.

Interview performance self-rating

Next, think about the following criteria to evaluate specific aspects of your interview performance. Rate your interview performance out of ten for each one of the criteria (1 = 'terrible and could do much, much better', 5 = 'average and could still do better', and 10 = 'perfect and did not for one moment go wrong'):

◆ *Research*. How would you rate your fact-finding and knowledge about the company? Did you know everything about the company, their industry, competitors, their strategy and structure? Did you also research the format of the interview and know exactly how many interviews and interviewers there would be at each stage?

◆ *Questions and answers*. How well did you respond to each of the questions that you were asked? Did you have good examples to show off your key qualities and skills? Were there any questions that you could have answered better?

◆ *Rapport with the interviewer*. Did you engage in polite conversation and put the interviewer at ease? Did you maintain a good posture throughout the interview? Did you use your tone of voice and body language to make the interviewer comfortable?

◆ *Your questions*. Did you ask sensible questions? Did those questions show that you were not only knowledgeable but also enthusiastic and motivated?

◆ *Follow-up letter*. Did your letter make good points about your skills and experience without tipping over the edge and becoming corny? You could even show a copy of the letter to your friends and ask them to comment on it.

Now go back through your scores. For any area that you scored less than 8 out of 10, think about what you could have done better.

FEEDBACK IS VITAL FOR IMPROVING YOUR INTERVIEW PERFORMANCE

The most valuable source of information about your interview performance comes directly from the interviewer. As soon as you have confirmation that you have been rejected, you should give the interviewer a call. While most interviewers are happy to spend five minutes on the telephone, relatively few are willing to give up their time to meet with unsuccessful candidates face-to-face.

Explain to the interviewer that feedback would be invaluable, as you would like to know what you could have done better. Be polite but persistent. Some questions to ask could include:

◆ "Did you have any concerns about my experience or CV?"
◆ "Were there any questions that you felt I didn't answer to your satisfaction?"
◆ "Do you have any suggestions as to what I could have done to make a better impression on you?"
◆ "Would you be able to tell me what the successful candidate did, or said, that helped him or her get the job over me?"

Many interviewers are loath to give negative feedback, but you should encourage the interviewer to be completely candid in giving you feedback. Emphasise again the fact that the feedback would help you to prepare more effectively for future interviews.

When the interviewer gives you any negative feedback, grit your teeth and keep smiling. Whether you agree or disagree is irrelevant. At this stage, it is very unlikely that you will be able to change the interviewer's mind. The interviewer has done you the favour of providing you with some honest feedback. So the least you can do is listen to it with good grace.

Only when you are off the telephone should you think about the feedback:

◆ Were there any pleasant surprises in the feedback?
◆ Were there any unpleasant shocks in the feedback and what should you therefore do differently in a future interview?

NEGOTIATE THE BEST POSSIBLE SALARY AND PACKAGE BEFORE ACCEPTING A JOB

It is a great feeling to be offered a job. After sifting through a pile of CVs and interviewing a shortlist of candidates, the employer has chosen you. Congratulations.

However, **resist the temptation to accept the offer immediately**. The employer wants you, but does not have you, which puts you in a privileged position. Now is the best time to try to negotiate a good salary and pay package. It is far more difficult to achieve pay rises and bonuses when you are working for an employer. Job changes provide most people with the best opportunity they will ever have to achieve a better deal at work. So ask now, or regret it later.

Set up a face-to-face meeting with the employer. Explain that you are pleased to have been made the offer, but that you have a few more questions to ask about the company before deciding whether to accept or not.

The following steps may help you to negotiate:

Estimate your worth

If you have been working for one employer for a number of years, your pay may be out of line with the going market rate. So check beforehand what someone of your experience could be making in other companies. To establish a realistic salary range, you could:

◆ Read job advertisements in the press.
◆ Talk to recruitment consultancies and headhunters.
◆ Look at salary surveys on recruitment websites.
◆ Ask friends and colleagues in similar lines of work.

Do not get too fixated on the salary. There are many other elements of a remuneration package that you should think about, such as:

◆ Pension contributions, medical benefits, life insurance, and other benefits.
◆ Season ticket loan, car allowance or company car.
◆ Bonuses, share options, or profit share.
◆ Gym membership and expense accounts.

◆ Payment of course tuition fees or time off to study for external exams.

◆ Mobile phone and laptop computer.

◆ Flexible working – such as the number of hours or days that you work a week, or the freedom to work from home on certain days.

Figure out your wants and needs

Negotiation is a process of trading off some of your superficial wants to achieve what you need. So prepare by thinking through the following questions:

◆ *What do you **want**?* In an ideal world, what would you like the employer to offer you?

◆ *What do you **need**?* In a more realistic world, what is the minimum that you are willing to accept from the employer? If the employer's offer is too low, you should have a lower limit in mind at which you will decline the job.

◆ *What benefits can you deliver to the employer?* Why should the employer give you what you want? What are your arguments going to be? What can you do for the employer to justify an increased pay package?

◆ *What minor concessions are you willing to make?* What would you be willing to give up or trade off to ensure that you get what you need? For example, you might be willing to put up with a smaller base salary for a bigger pension contribution and bonus.

Prepare to negotiate courteously

You have little to lose if you ask for a better deal. However, there is a big difference between asking and demanding.

Asking politely and listening to the employer's responses and reaching a compromise is acceptable to most employers, while demanding more in an aggressive manner could lead the employer to retract the job offer entirely. Giving ultimatums could appear adversarial and turn the employer off.

Wait for the employer to mention money

When you meet the employer, use the meeting as an opportunity to find out more about them. Ask questions to check whether this is a company that you would like to work for – for example, you might use this opportunity to ask further questions from Chapter 10. Avoid being the first to mention money – if you mention money too early on, the employer will think that you are motivated by money and little else.

The employer will eventually broach the subject, perhaps by asking you how much it would take to get you. If you possibly can, try to get the employer to mention a figure first. Negotiating a pay package is like playing poker – whoever reveals their hand first is in the weaker position.

If the figure is too low for your liking, try to *express your desire for more by selling the benefits that the employer would gain by employing you* – for example: "I would have thought that with my IT skills, I'd be worth more than that." Then put the pressure back on the employer with a question: "Do you think that's reasonable?"

But don't forget to offer up some concessions while negotiating too.

Get it in writing

Once you and the employer have reached an agreement, ask for a letter to confirm the details in writing. It does not have to be a formal contract – just a letter outlining all of your terms of employment. Receiving an offer in writing avoids mistakes or misunderstandings later.

WEIGH UP YOUR JOB OFFER BEFORE ACCEPTING

Looking for a new job is a stressful process. Just because you have a financially beneficial offer on the table may not mean that you will be happy. More pay could just mean longer hours, more travel, or a tougher working environment.

Before you accept that job offer, consider the following questions carefully:

◆ Do you like the work itself? Would you find the job sufficiently challenging or interesting?

◆ Are you happy with your prospective boss? Have you met and talked about the sorts of targets that you would have to achieve? Does your boss strike you as the sort of person that you would get on with? If you felt uncomfortable being interviewed for only an hour by your prospective boss, how would you feel about working together for several years?

◆ Do you like your prospective colleagues? Would you be able to work and socialise with them?

◆ Do you understand the politics of the organisation? And are you comfortable with the company's culture?

◆ Do you understand your future prospects in the company?

If your honest answers to those questions are "yes", then this really is the job for you. Write back to the employer to accept that job and then go celebrate. Well done!

SUMMARY

◆ Record basic details about your interview to help you remember whether you would actually want the job or not.

◆ Recognise that you will not get every job you interview for – but don't let it get you down.

◆ Evaluate your performance in every interview to learn and improve.

◆ Ask the interviewer politely for feedback. But make sure that you take it on board.

◆ Estimate your worth and be prepared to prove why you are worth more before asking for a better package.

◆ Think about the job. Just because you have an offer does not mean that you must take it. Will the job fulfil your personal and professional needs?

◆ Finally, if you have any observations about interview questions, interviewers or assessment centres – let me know: robyeung@robyeung.freeserve.co.uk

Further Reading from How To Books

CVs for High Flyers, Rachel Bishop-Firth, 2002

High Powered CVs, Rachel Bishop-Firth, 2002

Planning a Career Change, Judith Johnstone, 2002

The Internet Job Search Handbook, Andrea Semple and Matt Haig, 2001

The Ten Career Commandments, Rob Yeung, 2002

Returning to Work, 2nd edition, Sally Longson, 2002

Write a Great CV, Paul McGee, 2002

For comprehensive information on How To Books' titles visit How To Books on line at www.howtobooks.co.uk

Index

If you want to know how . . .

- To buy a home in the sun, and let it out
- To move overseas, and work well with the people who live there
- To get the job you want, in the career you like
- To plan a wedding, and make the Best Man`s speech
- To build your own home, or manage a conversion
- To buy and sell houses, and make money from doing so
- To gain new skills and learning, at a later time in life
- To empower yourself, and improve your lifestyle
- To start your own business, and run it profitably
- To prepare for your retirement, and generate a pension
- To improve your English, or write a PhD
- To be a more effective manager, and a good communicator
- To write a book, and get it published

If you want to know how to do all these things and much, much more . . .

howtobooks

Practical books that inspire

If you want to know how . . . to write a CV that works

"We have all faced the frustration of knowing we can do the job, but how do we get 'a foot in the door?' Your CV is the key to opening those doors. In this book you will learn not just how to sell yourself, but how to tailor and vary your approach accordingly. Interviews will also take on a new meaning when we see the role our CV typically plays in that situation."

Paul McGee

Writing a CV that Works
A concise, clear and comprehensive guide to writing an effective CV
Paul McGee

"This is one of the best guides I have come across which is aimed squarely at the UK rather than US user." – *A reader from London*

"A helpful book which draws out the essentials of what the CV writer will need to know about themselves. Helps the writer structure the information for best effect." – *A UK reader*

"*Career Focus* recommends *Writing a CV that Works*." – *Ms London Weekly*

ISBN 1 85703 365 5

If you want to know how . . . to write a winning CV

"Employers want to see what you can offer; they want to see it presented quickly and simply. And they want to see it in a format that is good for them to process through their recruitment procedures. A little research can not only make a CV look good, but can also make it pass quickly to the right person, getting you the opportunity to interview and make a personal impression, showing employers why they should hire you, and allowing you to decide whether you really do want to work for them."

Julie-Ann Amos

Write a Winning CV
Essential CV writing skills that will get you the job you want
Julie-Ann Amos

"If you are in the market for advice, *Write a Winning CV* is a great starting point." – *The Guardian*

"There is no shortage of publications concerning CVs and covering letters; so what has this new contender got to offer? Quite a lot, as it turns out. For a start it is written not by a careers adviser, but by a recruitment specialist . . . it is up-to-date, written with authority and packed full of helpful advice." – *N. Evans, Occupational Psychologist, Newscheck*

ISBN 1 85703 840 1

If you want to know how . . . to successfully apply for a job

"Being successful in a fiercely competitive jobs market takes time and effort. Spurring a recruiter into wanting to know more about you is the secret of success with any application. Each one must be special: it has to say – 'Here I am. This is what I can offer you.' This book is designed to help you present your skills in a practical and marketable manner and ultimately achieve your goal. How you approach this crucial first stage is vitally important, only successful applications lead to interviews."

Judith Johnstone

The Job Application Handbook
A systematic guide to applying for a job
Judith Johnstone

Whether you're leaving university, re-entering the job market, facing redundancy or simply wanting a change, this handbook reveals the best ways to approach potential employers.

ISBN 1 85703 992 0

If you want to know how . . . to change your career for the better

"We owe it to ourselves and to our families to find rewarding careers as part of a balanced life. A successful career move involves people matching their ideas, passions and goals to the needs of employers and vice versa. People need jobs and jobs need people. This book is to help people take a new look at themselves and supply them with the tools they need to make their career move – to a place where they can satisfy most of their needs and some of their wants. Whatever move you want to make it has to start from a basis of self-knowledge. An understanding of your needs and wants, and knowledge of what you can contribute.

There is a secret to successful job search. It is persistence. Seek and you shall find."

Graham Green

The Career Change Handbook
Find out what you're good at and enjoy; and get someone to pay you for it. It's as simple and as difficult as that
Graham Green

"Interesting and to the point advice." – *The Guardian*

"There is little of the silly and trivial advice often found in career advice books. *The Career Change Handbook* gives incisive advice." – *Tyrone Times*

ISBN 1 85703 865 7

How To Books are available through all good bookshops, or you can order direct from us through Grantham Book Services.

Tel: +44 (0)1476 541080
Fax: +44 (0)1476 541061
Email: orders@gbs.tbs-ltd.co.uk

Or via our website

www.howtobooks.co.uk

To order via any of these methods please quote the title(s) of the book(s) and your credit card number together with its expiry date.

For further information about our books and catalogue, please contact:

How To Books
3 Newtec Place
Magdalen Road
Oxford OX4 1RE

Visit our web site at

www.howtobooks.co.uk

Or you can contact us by email at info@howtobooks.co.uk